DUPED

BARELY A CHRISTIAN WITH SOME OF THE BENEFITS

ROBERT LAFLIN & TERRY JENSEN

ACW Press
Eugene, Oregon 97405

Scripture quotations are taken from the King James Version of the Bible.

DUPED! (Barely a Christian with some of the benefits)
Copyright ©2003 Robert Laflin and Terry Jensen
All rights reserved

Cover Design by Alpha Advertising
Interior design by Pine Hill Graphics

Packaged by ACW Press
85334 Lorane Hwy
Eugene, Oregon 97405
www.acwpress.com
The views expressed or implied in this work do not necessarily reflect those of
ACW Press. Ultimate design, content, and editorial accuracy of this work is the
responsibility of the author(s).

Library of Congress Cataloging-in-Publication Data
(Provided by Quality Books Inc.)

Laflin, Robert.
    Duped : (barely a Christian with some of the
benefits) / Robert Laflin and Terry Jensen.
    p. cm.
    ISBN 1-932124-06-3

    1. Christian life. 2. Discernment (Christian
theology) 3. Self-deception--Religious aspects--
Christianity. 4. Hypocrisy--Religious aspects--
Christianity. I. Jensen, Terry. II. Title.

BV4509.5.L34 2003   248.4
                                   QBI33-1191

Printed in the United States of America.

TABLE OF CONTENTS

FOREWORD

What started out as a magician's perspective on the mechanics of magic and its influence on people has ended up an in-depth study on the subject of deception and how it relates to the church. We offer the following perspective in hopes that the reader will come away with a greater understanding of the obstacles we encounter as we seek true discipleship. Our desire is that those who take the time and effort to study this work would see truth bleeding through the pages of it by the Holy Spirit of God, who leads us to truth. "But when He, the Spirit of truth comes, He will guide you into all truth." (John 16:13)

—Dr. R.A. Laflin

*S*omewhere between P.T. Barnum's philosophy "There's a sucker born every minute" and Jesus Christ's declaration in John 8:32, "You shall know the truth and the truth shall set you free" lies a large segment of human society that has bought into a lifestyle that seems right, safe, and secure. They live in a fog of deception while truth is put on the back burner waiting for another generation to rise up with spiritual discernment and declare with Job, "I have heard of you with the hearing of the ear, but now my eyes see you and therefore I abhor myself and repent in dust and ashes."[1]

The Allegory of Joe

Joe was a dreamer, born at a time and place that seemed to aid his anxious yearning to explore and conquer all he saw and desired. I always knew he would be special. As soon as I saw him, I knew he was perfect for me. Joe was just what I had wanted.

I was a friend to people, and so people liked being around me. My pretty smile, sincere laugh, and contagious energy brought out the best of everybody, so I rode the success of my ways. I was aware that I had listened with my feelings for the better part of my seventy-two years, but it was only now that I realized how many things I thought I had heard said that had never been spoken. I'll never forget the night my world was reinvented, not because of the death I had just witnessed, but because of the meaning of the words I had just grasped...

It began fifty-three years ago when Joe Smith married Sally Jones, taking the vows to love and cherish each other "as long as they both shall live." Joe didn't know what he was saying, and Sally had inadvertently heard something that Joe had never said. You see, actually Joe loved pornography. He cherished the possibilities of tomorrow while living for himself. Within the context of the vows they had just exchanged, Sally thought she had heard that she was getting security and romance in exchange for "just being Sally."

You can imagine this baggage would compound the impact of the usual predictable problems of life, so as years exposed the unbearable, they sought out relief amongst a parade of authors, counselors, and friends.

Then one day Joe and Sally found God. Joe was the first to convert, attending a service that brought him to the understanding that humans commit sins. Joe admitted that he was no exception. With his face buried in his cupped hands, he began to think through the lifestyle that he had built for himself. He faced his guilt regarding selfishness, he sought relief from his bondage of lust, he regretted his treatment of Sally, and he mourned his lack of regard for Christ. That Sunday morning Joe raised his hand for salvation, believing with all of his heart that this would be a new start.

Sally had prayed lots of times for marriage relief, but having a better husband was more than she expected. Eager to start afresh as well, she prayed the sinner's prayer the following week, and they were both baptized together on Wednesday.

The church stood to their feet and cheered as the drenched couple joined hands and left the baptismal together, but Sally and Joe's minds were a mile away that night. Sally felt she heard a brand-new husband sloshing to the changing room while Joe thought the corner market's filthy video tapes would no longer be his temptation.

As usual, Joe and Sally's circle of friends began to change. They met many mature Christians at church and were often invited to religious functions. Joe listened to all that his new friends had to say, observing their actions, taking in their testimonies, and mimicking their public behavior. Sally attended the women's Bible studies and ladies' luncheons. At first she was curious why so many women were requesting prayer for their marriages, but after a while she began to feel comfortable enough to admit that her marriage needed prayer too.

The years passed as Sally and Joe became familiar with the standards of their church, the doctrines of their faith, and the behavior that they were told pleased God. Joe became excellent at the discipline necessary to avoid most pornography and believed that maturing as a Christian seemed to be defined as humbly concealing one's condescending thoughts towards the church's "part-timers."

The best times they had usually involved their daughter, Sue. She survived an unknown bone disease for five years. By the time she died at the age ten, she had asked Jesus into her heart and had memorized the Twenty-third Psalm. Sue always wanted to know when she would be healed, the doctors wanted to know what was killing her, while Sally and Joe just wanted to know, "Why?"

The best religious experiences Sally and Joe shared together usually involved a pastoral "cheerleader" during church worship time or the occasional guest speaker. Sometimes they watched the religious channel together, but in general, family devotions were awkward. While the sum total definition of their religious life could not be called victorious, probably the term *disciplined* comes to mind. By observing cause and effect, it was apparent that for them, life always has its ups and downs.

Joe's worst times were those nights his mind would conjure up the thought that maybe his Christian mentors were not as confident about this religious lifestyle as they had led him to believe. What if the people he had trusted to disciple him were wrong? His mentors occasionally worked at the mission but didn't really know the men there. Joe trusted Christians who spoke with knowledge of Scripture, yet two of the deacon's sons had bad reputations in the youth group, and while his mentors answered most of his questions, the hard ones were always deferred to the answer that "We'll know when we get to heaven." Beneath it all there seemed to be this supernatural all-knowing final authority over everybody at church, reverently referred to as "the denominational headquarters."

Sometimes Sally dreaded the future. It seemed to her that before their salvation Joe and she had at least subconsciously agreed to exchange his provision of her security for her support of his ego. What had happened to that? He was popular at church, people noticed him, and he was an admired elder now. Maybe he didn't need her supporting his male ego any longer. How unfair! She still needed his security, she was the weaker vessel, what about all of her insecurities? Who else could she confide to that:

"I've never read my Bible all the way through because it's boring. In fact all that I know comes from people to whom I have trusted with all my religious beliefs: authors, pastors, and friends. God never says anything to me, I seldom really feel saved, I live on hope and promises, I wonder how much does God care. I wish God would give me a midterm report card! I wish I never married Joe, Kevin treats his wife like a queen, I want him! How come Avis is the only one who gets healed at prayer meetings every week—it seems that God has saved her a fortune on aspirins by healing her headaches every Wednesday—but we buried a ten-year-old "angel"? Why don't we just play the sermons of the television superstars on Sunday, since nobody remembers what pastor says anyway? If there is so much power in the blood, how come last night's television lineup featuring the psychic hotline and amazing videos demonstrated more supernatural forces than Sunday morning's testimonies. And by the way, if God is so unpredictable, how come all of our religious counseling always sounds the same? When is that evangelist coming back? I need a spiritual jump-start again."

Scared that a divorce would be a permanent monument to their individual selfishness, Sally and Joe stayed married.

Dutifully, they continued to perform to the standards of their church, crediting God with their attrition. The years saw Joe's personal problems peak and valley with his job pressures and secret temptations. Meanwhile, Sally's emotions swung from the ability to give wise council to the shame of her hidden fragile limits. However, by the time they were retired, both were the very "pillars of the faith" many of the new converts in their church were striving to emulate.

Now finding himself in his mid-seventies, the most honest introspection since his conversion would face Joe: he was dying. The combination of being a "pillar of the faith" and the fact that he was lying in the local hospital with perhaps only hours to live made Joe wonder: "What does my life mean to the people who are watching me die?"

He knew that Christianity had given him a direction and hope of a victorious lifestyle. He knew that the world did not have anything better to offer. He knew that he certainly would not have stayed married, sober, or responsible without the disciplines inherent to his religion. He knew he could have done better, he could have tried harder. Maybe if he had done more, his marriage and friendships and witness would have brought him closer to God. But Joe also knew that something was not right. All of those things were offered within most of the major religions. Faith, lifestyle, hope, help, and discipline: if that was all he had gleaned from Christianity, he might as well have been a Buddhist!

Joe was weak, he was losing consciousness, he felt his wife's hand squeeze his. She must have sensed him slipping. His last thoughts were questions: "Isn't being a Christian more credible than a Buddhist? Buddhists don't have the benefits of a living God. Why, I remember when God came down and...no, no that's not right, I had only wished He came down, but, but...well Buddha couldn't take away my pornography addiction as quick as God did, why, I beat that problem almost three month's ago…almost." Joe struggled to think of just one experience that Christianity did not just offer, but actually demonstrated, a single earthly evidence he could die knowing was unique to being a son of the LIVING GOD. Would it be power? No! Maybe two-way conversations? Not really. An out-of-body experience, a voice from a burning bush, a blinding light from heaven? NO!

Horror struck Joe's soul as a visual flashback to the night of his conversion overlaid his life. The commitment he had to God made the night he was saved had been born out of a supernatural revelation, a revelation that he had responded to by talking right from his heart directly to God, just a simple prayer. Intimate communication just seemed to spill from Joe's soul that night. What had happened that caused his prayers to evolve into a presentation of organized thoughts? It was so long ago, but now it seemed like yesterday. He had lost his first love. Being in love with God had turned into a lifestyle of doing things to achieve acceptance and appease his conscience. He had struggled his entire life to meet the requirements of the Scriptures but had never focused on just loving and knowing God. Joe was the prodigal son who had come home with his hand out, not his head hung. He struggled to open his eyes and there, still holding his hand, was Sally.

His voice was barely recognizable, it was only a whisper, but still he managed to breathe out a scripture he had never before understood: *"We have searched the scriptures hoping to find life, but we've failed to come to Jesus and have it."*

"He's talking, he's talking!" Sally was so excited all she could say was "he's talking!"

"What did he say?" the nurse asked.

Sally leaned forward. "What, sweetheart? What did you say?"

Peace engulfed Joe's face and as it fell to neutral he smiled. Using Sally's hand to help himself sit up straight, a strength came into his being where strength did not exist. Joe's eyes pleaded for her to understand his final breath. Could Sal hear with her heart just one more time? Could she decipher what will not be said? "Sweetheart," he sighed, "I've been duped…barely a Christian with just some of the benefits."

She heard him, she heard with her heart that which had not been said. Sally now knew and understood the Bible verse he had moments before whispered to her. *"We have searched the Scriptures hoping to find life, but we've failed to come to Jesus and have it,"*[2] Words that penetrated seventy-two years of patterns, quickened inside her by a patient and ever faithful LIVING SAVIOR. "I was changed the night Joe, my husband, died."

Joe was a dreamer, born at a time and place that seemed to aid his anxious yearning to explore and conquer all he saw and desired. I always knew he would be special. Who would have guessed he would have to die to achieve it?

CHAPTER ONE

Shema on You!

There's a problem with the church in America today, and even the greatest scholars and the most sincere pastors cannot seem to fix it. They can make it look OK for a while. They can make it seem to succeed, and it can affect people for good, but the truth is that the church in America still does far too many things wrong. Wrong, because the church "system" in its attempt to evangelize, educate, and equip is inadvertently replacing something we have always needed to find within ourselves: a personal direction and vision.

We do not intend to place the fault upon the church, on individuals, or even point a finger at the easy thing to blame: sin. We do not believe that Christians are the problem. In fact, God intends us to be a part of His solution to the human dilemma. The authors hope that as you read the following pages you will see that we do not make light of sin or the responsibility of each of us to respond to it. Neither do we underestimate the overcoming power of God's Holy Spirit. However, there has been very little written regarding the vulnerability of our five senses to earthly spiritual influences. If Christians could just see clearly, hear directly, and stay focused without these earthly influences, we do have the tools to defeat sin and to abide in God's direction. But clarity, focus and direction are not part of Satan's plan for mankind. As Ephesians 6:12 informs us; "We wrestle not against flesh and blood, but against principalities, against powers, against the rulers of the darkness of this world, against spiritual wickedness in high place." In short, we wrestle with Satan, who is allowed to operate on earth unseen, and his means of influence are also invisibly devastating.

This is not a thesis on evil. Our little opening story about Joe was meant to paint a visual picture of the Christian's struggle for victory after salvation. Joe's story was not a story of demon possession or uncontrollable spirits. Joe did not wrestle with a demon, but like all of us, Joe struggled with his circumstances. Circumstances that included his physical environment and his experiences. Joe's struggle to accurately interpret his circum-stance and then react appropriately is common to all mankind. Herein lies our precept: Satan's best attack on Christians and the Christian church is not an attack on our circumstances as much as it is an attack on our *perceptions* of our circumstances.

Whatever authority Satan has over Christians, Christians allow him to have. Therefore, the authors submit that perhaps Satan's best strategy is one he has always used to gain a say in our lives. Since Satan's attack against God's decrees and God's man-dates are futile, he must attack the weakest link in God's plan. And the weakest link in God's plan is man's free choice. Who would suspect that while blatant evil was ravaging mankind, Satan could infiltrate God's own "chosen" from the inside out?

Jeremiah saw that man's free choice was really not so free after all, if man does not have access to the truth. So perhaps we should start at the beginning and explain in detail what this all means to Christians today. Please do not jump to conclusions just yet, Deception is a hard concept to follow accurately. This is precisely what makes deception the most powerful weapon in the universe against truth!

For centuries mankind has sought to know the truth about life, eternity, and God. Adam probably sought it out while coming back to the Garden and facing a flaming sword. Jacob was looking for it while wrestling with the Angel of the Lord. Moses sought after truth in the harshness of the desert, and Pilate revealed his quest, asking Jesus himself, "What is truth?"

From early seekers such as Justin Martyr, Eusebius, and Augustine to Calvin, Wesley, and us, truth seems elusive. We find ourselves wondering, how much truth is possible for us to know and how much truth is necessary? What are the conditions and how is truth measured? This book is a simple study of what we perceive as *the* problem in the church today: the lack of truth. Adam and Eve were deceived *before* they sinned; yes, they seemed to have missed even obvious truth. Their story is a story of two people deceived into sinning, not forced into it. In fact, all sin in one way or another is a result of deception. But deception does not stop there. We insist that deception is also responsible for bad choices, misdirected efforts, lost opportunities, apathy, depression, frustration, mistakes, and many other problems that may not result in sin. The church in America today needs truth, and it is by definition that deception will always keep truth away.

God has never made a secret of the details regarding the truth He intended us to know. God's most basic requirement to His people has always been highlighted as the foundation of all truth. In fact, it is the pillar of Christian obligation,[3] known as the *Shema Yisrael,* and it reminds us of our Jewish roots revealed within the background of the Old Testament. The *Shema* is a beacon of truth, and we will refer to it often as our only hope to escape the influences of deception. It is said that the *Shema* "has been deeply imbedded in the consciousness of Jews however far they may be from the traditions of their faith."[4] "It is Judaism's greatest contribution to the religious thought of mankind,"[5] "the source from which Judaism time and again drew its strength for inspiration and rejuvenation."[6] The *Shema* derived its importance both from its intrinsic meaning and from the place it assumed in Jewish liturgy and history. Repeated morning and night, as well as in moments of gravest crisis and at death's door, it has sustained every generation of Jew.[7]

Here is the *Shema*: "Hear, O Israel: The LORD our God, the LORD is one. Love the LORD your God with all your heart and with all your soul and with all your strength. These commandments that I give you today are to be upon your hearts. Impress them on your children. Talk about them when you sit at home and when you walk along the road, when you lie down and when you get up. Tie them as symbols on your hands and bind them on your foreheads. Write them on the doorframes of your houses and on your gates" (Deuteronomy 6:4-9).

Notice how important God believes loving JUST Him is! We are to know it, do it, think it, believe it deeply, use our strength towards it, keep it, breed it into our families, and even talk about loving Him, everywhere and all of the time, and we are to proclaim it, on our hands, heads, houses, and communities! Some scholars believe that the book of Deuteronomy began here with the *Shema*,[8] right here with these six little verses, six little verses that rocked the world.

If these verses seem to be making a big fuss about nothing, then the reader needs to reread just what the "fuss" is all about. These "six little verses" were about to escort the Jewish world into a tragic history of intercessory priests, good and bad kings, bloody wars, thirteen judges, and through seven apostasies that were all predicted by countless prophets over fifteen centuries. Every single person and historical event would tell the story of

Israel's adherence to or departure from these "six little verses." And so will our lives today.

The story climaxes as Jeremiah, "the weeping prophet," solves the mystery of the illusive Shema. The solution to the mystery begins with some terrible news. Identifying Israel's enemy as Babylon, he suggests that Israel surrender, since God's judgment has already been determined for them.

Seven times Jeremiah is recorded as reporting to his people, "The imaginations of your hearts have deceived you." He informs them that the heart is deceitful above all things and desperately unchangeable, and they are powerless to know it. He takes God's chosen people down memory lane, highlighting their wholesale abandonment of the *Shema* for more than a thousand years. Here Jeremiah mans the curtain that would begin to draw on the final scene of the Old Covenant, and he proclaims the problem is deception!

Hundreds of years later we read in Romans chapter eleven, alluding to the significance of Jeremiah's message to God's chosen people, Paul explains the New Covenant. But as for Jeremiah's message, God has declared that Israel is about to be carried away into captivity, away from the Promised Land. If pagan culture is what they want, Babylon is what they shall have. Because of deception, a broken relationship would now insulate the majority of the "chosen people" from God, leaving only a remnant of obedient seekers with any hope of enjoying access to their Lord.

Somewhere between the land of Ur of the Chaldeans and Babylon, Israel had become misdirected from a relationship established between them and God. Blessed with a clear revelation and supernatural help through virtually every aspect of life, the vast majority of the "chosen people" of God had become "parrots," capable of reciting instructions and mimicking behavior. They learned to embrace deceptive influences as they searched the law hoping to find life, yet failed to commune with God and have it. Just like Adam and Eve, they were deceived.

Today these same influences may alter our understanding of God as well, and the results will produce the same tendencies for "parroting." God is supposed to be an *inside* influence (living being) and can offer unfathomable untapped potential within our lives if we can return to God's original and basic command: "Hear Oh Israel, the Lord is one Lord and you will love Him with of your heart, with all of your soul and all of your strength."

Deception has not changed in six thousand years. In the next few chapters, we will attempt to identify ten principles that ultimately define the deception that has us forging into "virtual Christianity." The principles include: equivoque, authority, disguise, suggestion, confusion, anticipation, ruse, misdirection, substitution, and repetition. Damage control from these ten principles of deception is almost nonexistent, for by the time the damage is revealed, it is usually too late, and we have hopelessly lost sight of the truth.

Truth begins and ends with the *Shema,* but we have been deceived. Deceived into replacing its requirement for a relationship with God with a struggle over finding God's will for us amidst an assortment of flesh-and-blood issues. The *Shema* serves as an ancient reminder and was even reiterated by Jesus so we can know, not guess, God's will for us. God is to be our focus. His message could not have been clearer or more consistent for the past six thousand years. Our reason for being is not a self-centered stroll across a limited span of history. It is not to be ourselves, not our plans, not our dreams, and not our rights. Adam and Eve learned the hard way that Satan has always used the principles of deception to offer up a dangerous replacement for a personal relationship with God. Satan's version of Christianity offers reasonable ideas, but no life. It offers believing, but no faith. It offers help, but no sacrifice. It ultimately mis-defines "love." We call it virtual Christianity. Thanks to deception, virtual Christianity is alive and well in many a Christian person, and ultimately it has appeared uninvited within the American church today.

CHAPTER TWO

Broken Wands and Magic Spells

(If wishes were horses, beggars would ride)

His eyes penetrated the smoky room almost like black embers on gray paper. His jaw was set, and his face was as leathery stone. There was a reverence honored by his presence, and as he slid the metal chair to the head of the table, we all subconsciously leaned forward to witness another "miracle." He ground out his cigarette on a bottle cap and brushed the ashes to the floor. His arrogance for perfection, coupled with his implied challenge "to find him out," could not be ignored. The fifteen or so onlookers were under a spell, and had paid good money to be so. Tonight, here on the fifth floor of an abandoned bookstore in Seattle, Washington, our destinies may well be touched.

I had seen his type before, once in 1973, in Gardiner, Montana, inside the Two Bit Saloon. The cowboy bar cheered as he entered, and I (T.J.), an eighteen-year-old kid, witnessed that same "spell." "Rick's here!" "Rick's here!" I heard. I watched him come through the very door that at one time served as Gardiner's only jailhouse. He was no cowboy; Rick was wearing brown slacks and a white shirt and tie. He was about thirty years old, six feet something, and had a cigarette half smoked as the door closed. I was just passing through, but everybody here knew Rick. I seemed to be the only one in the place who didn't know what was about to happen. The crowd parted, making a path for him to the center of the room where a pool table served as his ashtray. Flicking his ashes onto the felt, he pushed them into a pile and then turned to the "prettiest gal" in the place and, speaking for the first time, said, "Will you help me?"

I only recall her hands, no nail polish, but long slender fingers with a light complexion holding them out in front of her as if sleep walking. "Please, close your hands," he said. "And keep them closed." You could almost hear the entire bar inhale as he touched the ashes from the pool table onto the back of her hands. Slowly he rubbed the ashes into her skin, whispering something that sounded a lot like his telephone number, until no trace of the ash was left.

Rick backed away and lit up another cigarette. He allowed far too long to let what had just happened sink in, but in 1973, in Gardiner, Montana, at ten o'clock at night there wasn't one person in fifty who had anything better to do than wait, and so we did. It was only about a minute, I suppose, before Rick blew a long drag of smoke across the back of the girl's outstretched fists, and with the same penetrating eyes I would see ten years later, he suggested to us all that we were about to witness a "miracle."

As I look back on these two momentous occasions in my life, I now realize that the dramatic influence these people had on me came from the fact that they had something I wanted. These men were exciting. Like most people, I was looking to others for something worth having in my own life, and through these two events, my life's vision focused onto "life enhancers," misdirecting me from "life answers." The vision for my life was established by two men I chose to emulate, and everything else in my life would be "made to fit." I wasn't involved with evil, but I was not involved with God either.

I now realize with some embarrassment that nothing they or I would have to offer possessed any eternal value. I recall the guy in the bookstore wound up vanishing some paper using misdirection, and Rick had slipped ashes onto the girl's palms without anybody catching him. Two silly little tricks, found in many dime store novelty books had captured the fascination of an impressionable youth and sent me on a quest of nonsense for more than twenty years.

One of the greatest athletes of our time, Sydney Howard, observed that one half of knowing what you want is knowing what you must sacrifice to get it.[9] This echoes Jesus' admonition to an anxious follower recorded in Scripture. Jesus exposed the rich man's true desires by asking him to sacrifice his riches. The rich man learned his own heart that day and walked away sadly acknowledging his choice. A wrong road does not eventually become right. If we are fortunate enough to realize our wrong road, we must choose to make it right. And sustaining one's direction on right roads will require great sacrifice. It certainly did for me.

The process of thinking about your goals without any intention of paying the price to see them through to fruition is called wishing. It is not called planning. It is easy to find people who plan their lives without ever assessing the effort necessary to achieve their desires. The department of student loans in almost every college across America can testify to the accuracy of this prediction. Their experience regarding uncollected tuition from unmotivated dropouts punctuates the distinction between planning to graduate and wishing to graduate. This is deception territory. The quest for truth is an arduous path, and our commitment to it must not be a wish, but a God-given desire. Without this commitment, without the surrender of our choices to this commitment, deception will win. We will wind up committing our lives to the wrong things.

Satan understands his opportunities within your "cocktail of life." The ingredients include blending some combination for living out of: goals, wills, destinies, purposes, desires, plans, visions, abilities, choices, and motivation. Can you see how these ingredients were used to misdirect a "foolish seeker" through a mysterious stranger, a smoky room with a pretty girl and a "magical" happening? Deception is the "swizzle" stick for the cocktail of our lives. Here Satan has an opportunity to introduce you to the "principalities and powers" he needs to invite himself to your house.

Deception is well at home in anybody who bases their desire on happiness, wealth, success, or any other self-directed pleasure. Deception loves to offer purpose. It breeds confused motivations and sits as the authority of our will. And so it goes, through each ingredient of life, deception influences the destiny of our lives while damaging the effectiveness of God's church.

How can we avoid repeating the failures of Israel as recorded in the Old Testament, winding up with just a form of religion? What hope do we have to begin our life without corruption? How do we let God lead us in a practical and real way? Do we submit ourselves to a person or institution that knows more than we do? Can we find a pattern or tradition that ingrains proper behavior in our lives? Do we just choose as best we can, given our limited understanding? What will be our plan to avoid the misdirection and confusion of life? How can we as Christians be assured of our destiny and live with contentment in our present?

Can we trust God to really deliver something better? Must we pretend, or does God really mean it when He invites "whosoever will" into a company of believers to enjoy a personal relationship with Him through a life led? We submit that to achieve a victorious destiny on any level, God's plan must become our plan.

Unfortunately, Satan has a plan for your life too. He wants you to die without God, to die without ever considering the love of God or hearing the gospel. If you do hear the gospel, then he does not want you to believe it. If Satan is unsuccessful at keeping you from believing the gospel, then he does not want you to accept it. Certainly Satan does not want you to live out the requirements of the *Shema* to "love him" successfully. At all cost Satan cannot let you disciple others as Jesus commanded.[10] If you listen close enough, you can almost hear Satan slide a spiritual easy chair and a warm blanket in your direction. "Have a seat," he invites. "Make yourself comfortable, Mr. or Mrs. Christian. I'll be back to check on you." Satan redefines the Christian life for us through our various encounters with the ten principles of deception, and he hides our need for Christ from us.

In Satan's domain truth is disguised, misdirected, substituted, confused, dulled, and subtly controlled through influences inherent to a fallen world.[11] Truth is deceptively manipulated as we rub elbows with a fallen people and grow old, exposing our heart to a spiritual environment that our five senses are powerless to discern.

Just as silence is the absence of sound, as cold is the absence of heat, as darkness is the absence of light, as evil is the absence of good, so deception is the absence of truth. Satan's plan is the easy plan. It happens automatically when you invent your own ideas of what God requires of you—just ask Israel.

Deception offers an answer that *almost* satisfies. It will probably seem right because we have tailored it to fit ourselves. What danger we expose ourselves to when we mix our own desires with an assortment of "Christian teaching" and occasional prayer with a dab of comfortable sacrifice! We admit you may not wind up with a philosophy that is evil, but it is never the truth. Deception is Satan's plan for you every single day. "Come this way," it declares, "trust me."

CHAPTER THREE

The Circus
Comes to Town

*"I have built my empire on
the firmest ground that can
be found—the foolishness
of people"* Ivar Kreuger

Before we begin the specifics of the ten principles of deception, we think it may be wise to point out that these principles are "scientific." They are repeatable, observable, and demonstrable by anyone familiar with them.[12] The principles of deception are not "spirits," not powers, and are not evil by themselves. They do not only affect our spiritual lives and are not just destructive to our souls. Entertainers such as magicians use these principles all of the time when they utilize mirrors, "palm" a card, or flip a double-headed coin. The principles of deception are in play every time we forget who's talking, the ventriloquist or dummy. By definition women deceive every time they accent (or disguise) a facial feature with makeup. These ten principles of deception will ultimately be shown as a potential hidden horror of our Christian "system," but it is important to understand that the ten principles of deception are a fact of life, not a face of

27

Satan. They can be innocently applied as life "enhancement" or destructively manipulated by deceivers. Either way, we have become far too casual about the possibilities of deception.

Ivar Kreuger was born in Kalmar, Sweden, in 1880. He came to America in 1900, returned to Sweden in 1902, and shot himself in the heart in 1932, but not before he became the richest man in the world. On one rare occasion he granted an interview with the *Saturday Evening Post*. Reporter Isaac Marcosson recorded Ivar's tribute to his own success as follows, "Whatever success I have had may perhaps be attributed to three things: One is silence, the second is more silence, while the third is still more silence."[13]

Kreuger was a hermit type, not flamboyant or flashy, but he had grand desires and a will that would stop at nothing to obtain them. Shrouded in mystery, his silence was part of his strength. He was a pioneer in the match business: at one time, three out of every four matches available in the world were Kreuger's. Some historians have speculated that Ivar's contact with a syphilitic prostitute in Vera Cruz caused him to develop a paresis of the brain, resulting in his unrealistic fantasy to buy the world. However, nobody would know of his eccentric plan, one of the most brazen cons in history, until 750 million dollars (1912 dollars!) had been swindled from investors and his monopolies dominated every country in the world except Russia.[14]

His authority lay in his amazing ability to gain the complete confidence of one individual at a time and then transfer that relationship to a credible reputation. His reputation was bigger than reality, his knowledge of a specific industry (matches) credible, and his personality engaging. Igniting his abilities was nothing less than a vision: to make every match in the world. He planned to accomplish this by convincing rich people to believe in him, trust him, and help him. This would require deception because Ivar was not going to protect other people's welfare ahead of his own.

The risks would not be equally shared.[15] Faced with the question: "How do I get people to give me what I want?" Ivar understood that key people must be controlled by their choices.

Armed with one of the ten principles of deception—authority—along with the ability to predict other's desires and the wisdom of silence, Ivar Kreuger began his scheme by printing his own money! He made fake Italian bonds. Worthless paper that was disguised as currency, it was basically nothing that looked like something. Kreuger had fake collateral that he would parlay into real cash, capturing the attention of those who wanted what he seemed to be offering: power, prestige, and wealth.

Kreuger owned a holding company called Kreuger and Toll. Although it was just another Ivar "empty promise," he sold securities to millions of investors and paid extravagant dividends to the stockholders (25 to 30 percent annually from 1919 to 1928). The staggering dividends attracted additional investors, thereby providing more cash to be doled out as dividends. All the while, the holding company was collateralized by Ivar's worthless Italian bonds.

Misdirected by the money coming in as dividends, nobody paid any attention to the actual value of Kreuger's empire. Because of the seemingly endless profits he could generate, it was reported that New York bankers would meet him with money in their hands at customs whenever he would come to the U.S.[16] Country after country was misdirected by the benefits they received from Kreuger's scheme. History records that nobody even suspected him, simply because nobody realized that there was something to catch.

Silently, Kreuger watched as his victims revealed their desires, hinting to Ivar how they should be "played." Silently, Ivar caused the matches on the store shelves to change names. Silently, Ivar Kreuger hid his deceit and avoided any personal commitments that could reveal his weaknesses. Silence, silence, and more silence strengthened Ivar's position as he allowed his unwitting followers to do his bidding. His companies appeared to be poster children for credibility. He placed select people in the lead roles of each company's divisions for a reason that would only become apparent through the historical reconstruction of the fall of the Ivar Kreuger match empire.

Dukes and lords, as well as others with established positions or titles, loaned their credibility to Kreuger. He chose people to manage his companies, not because of their skill or knowledge, but because of their reputations. His management "team" suggested that Ivar's newly formed companies were founded and controlled from the deepest roots of tradition and credibility. Who would suspect such a rapid growth was "fishy" from observing this group? What bank dare audit such power? Who would suspect "silent" Kreuger while he was the least noticeable of these "captains of industry"?

Ivar had established himself as an *authority*, the fellow who (it seemed) could deliver other people's dreams. He did it by *disguising* himself (and credentials). He would appear to be something he wasn't. His assets would appear to be significant. He would appear to be credible.

Implementing his scheme during an era of poor communications and rapid growth, *confusion* kept his "rob-Peter to pay-Paul" method a secret. Silence, silence, silence offset the unsettling effects of *confusion*. Ivar let people's own assumption (*anticipation*) answer unanswered questions.

Behind this huge empire was a huge ego that was hidden by the classic *ruse*; the hidden motive was "hidden" because continued growth, tricky cash flow practices, and *substitution* (fake collateral) *misdirected* any seeker from "the bottom line."

Ivar Kreugar's silence, silence, silence as reported by the *Saturday Evening Post* was not only a character trait but good deception. Reporter Isaac Marcosson picked up on this silence and thought it was an interesting feature of a unique man, but this usual "red flag" was overlooked simply because it had become a pattern. Silence can be deafening. Silence when an answer is due, silence when trouble is on the horizon, or silence when victory is apparent should have been a warning sign. By repeatedly, consistently, and expectedly maintaining his silence, Ivar's silence became acceptable as the "norm."

After the crash of the stock market in1929, his bold lending and buying schemes began to collapse. Too many years of economic depression had apparently beat Kreuger by attrition. So it was that after traveling to Paris and locking himself inside his salubrious apartment he enjoyed a light dinner. Then a self-inflicted bullet to his chest caused Kreuger's empire to collapse to the floor along with his dead body.

In the following days and weeks, scores of his business associates would also end their lives. Bucking the trend, one powerful European banker was recorded, saying as he openly wept, "Although Ivar has ruined me and my banks, I cannot hate him. He was so charming and likable." It is small wonder he was given a hero's burial.[17]

Ivar Kreuger, the man who started the superstition "three on a match" just to sell more matches, has left a footprint in history that reflects the devastating pattern of human gullibility. He was a silent deceiver, acquiring the world by taking that which was and was not his. Ivar left his victims broke, some of them dead, and others happy just to know him. Not a person, friend or foe, not a government or government official, not an investor stupid or savvy, understood what had gone wrong. According to author Jay Nash, millions of people were ruined by one man's ability to hide the truth.[18]

America was well represented in the casualties. If you were a Christian living in America in 1932, you might have attributed much of this man's publicized painful fallout to Satan. But Satan can only be one place at a time, and too much credit goes to demons. Too little credit is attributed to our own common human vulnerabilities that make access for demons to go to work. The principles utilized by Ivar to con the world were not invented by him. The ten principles of deception have been around since Adam, utilized by women and polar bears, spirits and spies, and yes even Satan.

Do you think you could spot deception? Most people believe they can. Most believe they understand it and can avoid it with careful observation. Most people believe that deception is just a lie or sin inflicted upon them, not understanding it is actually a targeted influence. By definition, deception is impossible to "catch." If we could see deception in the making, then by definition we were not deceived; thus, no deception occurred. Spotting deception is like knowing you're asleep; if you know it, you're not.

Deception always hides the truth, and without truth deception is too well hidden to be recognized. The problem arises when we fail to understand what the lack of truth actually means to our beliefs. That if we have failed to acknowledge deception, then we only think we know the truth. "You could never con me!" is music to a con man's ears. Without exception, the louder the protest, the more "pluckable the pigeon."[19]

Ivar Kreuger is gone and forgotten, but the lessons his victims learned will be relearned by a new generation. These insights are not lessons on how to concoct a formula for a deception antidote, but a basic lesson in human nature. Mankind's condition was introduced to Israel by Jeremiah, "The heart is deceitful above all things,"[20] and we are once again reminded of this by a modern day anti-hero. Ivar Kreuger confirmed an inherent weakness common to all mankind, a weakness denied by the enlightened, ignored by the arrogant, laughed at by the apathetic, and redefined by the foolish. "Our hearts are deceitful above ALL things (even demons) and desperately UNCHANGEABLE, and we CANNOT know it. (try as we may)."[21]

Ivar's exploits may have been unique in their scope and effect, but his temptations, his perspective, and his death are very much common to mankind. His tragic story teaches a negative concept with a most depressing ending. Nothing says, "It's hopeless!" louder than a self-delivered bullet. Nothing is more hopeless than ignoring just how helpless we are.

Why study deception? First, because you cannot run from it, you cannot escape it, you cannot pretend it does not exist. Deception is part of the human condition, and to be ignorant of it is to be consumed by it. The darkest form of being deceived is when one claims that they aren't. Therefore, deception's goal is to make you confident of your own position and abilities. Our goal is to make you run toward Jesus with the knowledge of what is chasing you. Investing your life in Jesus is not just an ideal; it must be a reality if we are to benefit from God's protection. Always remember that raising your hand for salvation has gotten Satan's attention too.

Secondly, nobody invests their life in something that they do not believe in. Look around you and notice how people spend their time, and you will see what they believe. But believing something does not necessarily make it true and the deception of a false belief can only be spotted in the "rearview mirror." Deception becomes unveiled in time when what it has produced is lamented. Therefore, we want to help you to understand what it is you see in your "rearview mirror."

Finally, we study deception because it is not tangible, and it "morphs" to fit the situation. A hunter would not use a duck call to attract moose. He uses a moose call. Likewise, Satan looks like an angel of light to those looking for light, and he looks like nothing for those who look for nothing. Satan is the ultimate confidence man, and those not informed of his methods will always be on guard against the wrong things.

CHAPTER FOUR

Attending the
Funeral of Choice

Equivoque

A mid-sixteenth century innkeeper named Thomas Hobson owned a livery stable in Cambridge, England. He was determined that each of his forty horses would be equally exercised. No matter which horse his customers believed that they had selected from the list on the wall, they were always given the one closest to the door. It soon became known that the apparently free choice offered by Hobson was actually no choice at all.[22] This practice was and still is called "Hobson's Choice." A limited selection offered and then accepted without question will deliver a predictable outcome. One could say Hobson could predict the future. He could tell you today which horse would be the first one ridden tomorrow, but actually he simply manipulated the future by controlling people's choice. It is with this principle of Hobson's choice that we begin our study on deception.

Over the years Hobson's choice has been refined into a system that seems to predict the future and has become known in "deceiver's" circles as *equivoque*. We believe that as Christians our futures are beginning to look a lot like our pasts, and equivoque is a major reason.

People have some pretty strange ideas about the future. When I (Bob Laflin) found my place in a ministry that incorporated the spiritual gift of knowledge, I found myself answering practical questions about the future. Only God knows the future. Sometimes He reveals the future to us by "foretelling" the future with prophecy. Usually, the future revealed by God through prophecy that tells us of God's ultimate plans. In this case He invites us to choose to participate in what IS going to take place regardless of our choices. Prophecy reveals to us truths such as Jesus IS coming again, and the fact is that no human's choice is going to stop it from coming to pass.

Words of knowledge are usually more specific and are "forth-telling" more than "foretelling." Words of knowledge speak to our future or our present situation by encouraging us to make wise choices that will affect us individually. Sometimes that encouragement comes when God acknowledges our good choices, and sometimes it comes when God warns us of our bad choices. But forth-telling means that our choices will affect our future. What a blessing to hear from God as He speaks with knowledge about our own personal situations, and it is a privilege to serve God's people with this gift. But God does not always use prophets to lead, correct, or instruct His church. God the Holy Spirit indwells believers, and His power is available to any believer and will eventually be the means by which God perfects His church. So why isn't His church perfect now? One reason is equivoque, the principle of deception that tricks us out of our ability to choose rightly even in the midst of trying to follow God!

The "American lifestyle" offers us freedom to choose any lifestyle as long as it looks the same. It seems that we all need to own a car, a television, a telephone, a computer, a microwave, a stereo. We all believe in the concepts of fashion, vacation, retirement. We care about our success and our significance. We all worry about common things, our health, our safety, and our "stuff." It would seem that if Satan wanted a plan to diminish God in our lives, Satan would transfix our focus onto these things. And this is exactly what he does. He does it because it always works. Satan knows, after six thousand years of experience of watching mankind struggle to "balance" these lifestyle ideals amidst a personal relationship with God, failure is eminent. Eventually, the concept of "being" in a relationship with God becomes reduced to a relationship of "doing." It's predictable, because it's equivoque.

No matter how sloppy our Christian walk may become, we can always make time to "do" something that appeases our conscience for Christ. Slowly the "Christian life" is redefined. Expectations are lowered because perspectives change. We go through the motions of a personal relationship with God, but we secretly wish for a "sign" that we are where we are supposed to be. We are offered a list of options we can freely choose to "do" for God, but the list eventually wearies us. We have no idea what the apostle Paul meant when he stated "For me to live is Christ." The ability to seek God wanes, and the hope of "being changed into his likeness" by beholding His face (2 Corinthians 3:18) is lost.

A desperately thirsty man does not have to actually drink a glass of water to prove to himself that he greatly desires it. If he is thirsty enough, his entire being yearns so strongly that his focus is narrowed only to that glass of water. However, for the average person, drinking water is usually not a desperate quest but a minor urge. Likewise, a desperately sinful man may be focused on the only source of relief for his sin, God. Yet as time goes on (business having been taken care of), a relationship with God is often reduced to a minor urge. Though we are still able to "freely" choose God, the concept of "free" is really all relative to how we see our need. People with homemade "American" agendas can call on God until the cows come home, but time has prioritized our choices, and God is not fooled about our half of His relationship with us.

Equivoque is a principle of deception that "happens anyway." Equivoque offers the choice of no choice, because with each beat of your heart, a choice is either made by you or for you. Make your choice and other choices are automatic. You are God's "holy temple," or you are not. You are His "sheep" whom he will lead, a "servant" who will serve Him, a "priest" who will evangelize, or a "soldier" who will stand, or you are not.

Choices are not always made with our knowledge, and that is the essence of this principle of equivoque. It is not only our own agendas that feed this deception of choice of no choice; it is laziness, apathy, and lack of knowledge that breeds equivoque. We take the path of least resistance, we believe what we hear, we accept what we admire, and we seek what is most desirable among a list of options that may not have been assembled by God.

All of us need to learn to pray for direction and wisdom and access to good choices, not just the obvious ones. We must be careful not to advance our own agendas by misusing Scripture to support what we are predisposed to believe anyway. God led Israel personally until they wanted a king. How can God lead us, His "new Israel," if we still want to have kings, selfish agendas, or predisposed choices handed to us?

One guru of the modern computer age, Allen Kaye, said that "the best way to predict the future is to invent it." Utilizing equivoque, Hobson did exactly that by inventing the morning agenda of the horse closest to the door. Satan loves to watch us "default" to the path of least resistance too, because that is a predictable scenario Satan wants to see. Not unlike Hobson, there is a list on the wall, maybe not the names of horses, but a limited list that is placed in front of each one of us, and we are freely allowed to choose from it. What does your list say? Does it say things you like to hear or things you need to hear? Who hung up your list of choices? Was it Mr. Tradition, Mrs. Culture, or the successful church down the street?

By planting suggestions, limiting knowledge, offering eye "candy" playing to our desires and subtly forcing choices, the future for you can be and probably is manipulated. Equivoque creates a predictable future and features the principle of offering only wrong choices while all the time keeping us unaware that the best choices and certainly the right choice are never offered as an option.

Many people want to know the future. It is surprising how many people in and outside of the church want to know what lies ahead for them. What lies ahead for us all is death and judgment. What specifically lies ahead for anyone of us tomorrow depends on our choices. Satan knows that better than we do: he has watched mankind for six thousand years. Flip Wilson's popular phrase, "The devil made me do it" might better be put, "The devil helped me choose it," because our choices are influenced by the supernatural. We battle not against flesh and blood, but against principalities, against powers, against rules of darkness and spiritual wickedness in high places. We need supernatural help, but even here equivoque may control our choices.

It is human nature to be fascinated with the supernatural, and it has been my observation (B.L.) that people seeking an experience with "spirituality" instead of with Jesus are more fascinated with the *power* of forth-telling knowledge than with the personal touch of God to man. Seeking the gift, a miracle, or just information leads us away from Jesus, and we make bad choices pursuing that quest. I remember after one service in Seattle a woman came to me and said, " I really appreciated what you had to say. I know a lot of psychics like you." This woman missed the point of what she witnessed. She believed the power but chose to believe it was a "spiritual" wonder and not an act of God.

I remember sitting in a meeting with a pastor and two well-known authors when one of the men asked me what the difference was between what I do and any other psychic? I responded simply, "They aren't pointing people to Jesus." The words that Jesus speaks into people's lives live on into generations and have meaning that resonates as eternal words of life and not just information. God speaking into people's lives is part of the "deal." It is called a *relationship,* and you do not need a prophet to deliver one to you. You need to develop your own relationship with God. It takes time, your time. It takes focus, your focus. It takes a clear vision with determined choices, choices that will not be offered to you by equivoque.

Equivoque never offers Jesus. It may offer fascination and mystery, it might provoke imagination and curiosity, it might lead people (like Simon the sorcerer) to seeking it or promise direction, but it will never embrace one striving to live for Christ. Satan knows equivoque is most effective against Christians when it offers us everything that looks like Christ but not Christ Himself. These bad choices can be identified in hindsight because they were not a product of prayer. Instead, we will tend to measure their value with our feelings. Your freedom to choose is dead in the hands of this deception, and it got buried before you could say, "Thank you, Mr. Hobson!"

This should not lead us to believe that equivoque is just a mystical thing that must be accepted as a part of life. Like the other principles of deception, equivoque is a real thing that can be scientifically proven in accordance with the definition of science: it is a demonstrable, repeatable, and observable truth. Magicians are living proof that controlled choice is a principle of deception that can be packaged and presented at will:

"...and for my next trick I have handed an envelope to a gentleman in the audience. Will you stand? In that envelope is my prediction of which of these items lying on this table his wife will select. Madam, if you will bring any one of those four items to me, we will see if my prediction is correct."

The lady walks onto the stage, picks up an ice skate, and brings it to the entertainer. "Will you open the envelope please?" The paper reads, "SKATE," and the magician receives his applause.

This trick (as amazing as any entertainer could make it seem) was nothing more than predicting and then controlling human nature. It starts with selecting the right women. She must be dignified, intelligent, skeptical, and well dressed. A performer who cannot correctly identify this person should not be doing mentalism type tricks.[23]

The items on the table are not random choices. They are carefully placed items. On the left side of the table is placed a toilet plunger (Make sure the handle is damp.) To the center rear of the table is placed an extremely full glass of water. At the very front of the table is placed a beautiful red rose in a small pretty vase. On the right side of the table is placed a skate.

A dignified women does not want to touch, let alone carry, a wet who-knows-with- what plunger across the stage. A skeptical and intelligent person will not choose the obvious (rose). A well-dressed woman, preferably in a dress and heels, will not want to balance water in a glass on a stage that may already be slippery.

And so there sits a skate, easy to carry and unusual enough to be random. For this type of person, the skate is the forced choice. Everything works itself: thus equivoque has been utilized, yet nothing was random. Deception seems to be random, but it is a default from missing truth, and we miss truth because we fail to be led. Equivoque does not necessarily constitute an exchange of agreements through free will. It simply tests one's convictions while exposing our vulnerabilities and lusts.

Grace, healing, and forgiveness are concepts introduced to the human race by God. They give us hope that "all things work together for good for those who love God and are called according to His purpose."[24] These Christian concepts defeat the usual outcomes of "cause and effect." In fact, the Bible teaches that spiritual warfare will empower us to overcome a "cause and effect" lifestyle.[25] For instance, when Peter saw Jesus crucified, did this apparent defeat of Peter's "object of faith" cause him to doubt Jesus? The natural effect was that Peter went back to fishing for fish instead of fishing for men.

The men and women who had become the agents of Satan through the deception of their own lusts and assumptions had killed Jesus. For three days the disciples were silenced and the Christian hope defeated. Without overcoming the principles of deception, Satan would have won through controlling choice (equivoque). Judas chose money, the people chose Barabbas, Pilate chose popularity, Jesus chose silence, and Peter chose fishing…end of the story. Choices apart from the leading of God do not necessarily begin a predictable pattern that will end up where we thought they would end up.

But in the spiritual realm, unbeknownst to Peter, Jesus was battling death and sin according to God's plan. What an unpredictable end to the story we have! Jesus is raised from the dead, seeks out his friend Peter, restores his faith, and saves mankind from eternal damnation with the very object that was meant to destroy the plan of God, the cross.

In this story we learn a basic truth: deception will not defeat God. Peter's misunderstanding was exposed when deception was ultimately defeated and the early saints of the faith were restored to ministry. For all of its good, the church in America simply cannot offer the kind of leadership that it takes to pull us out of this kind of despair. It takes a spiritual power from a personal touch. Jesus touched Peter, and we have been left with no less than the "the Comforter" to "touch" our lives. This touch may be offered from the pulpits of our finest church institutions, but it will only be found in a personal commitment and sacrifice of the individual. It can only be realized through the help of the Holy Spirit working in an individual who seeks first to love God through obedience. WE must CHOOSE to love God with all of our heart and all of our soul and with all our strength. We must teach this love to our children because they want it, because they see it in our lives and upon our heads "and on our city gates"! Any other way we seek only offers us a form of truth with limited options and eventually defines our version of Christian faith. Equivoque offers the church in America today limited choices that have been hung on the wall by our own self interests. It offers us "virtual Christianity." And we should run from it!

CHAPTER FIVE

The Deputy's Diaper

Authority

He entered town slinging a gun. He wore it high on his hip, but it was tied unusually low on his leg. Most gunmen were bigger than life, but this fighter barely peered out of a ten-gallon hat with hollow eyes and clinched mouth. He didn't say a word as he parried down the dirt street shuffling his boots, leaving spur marks in the dust. Heads turned to stare at the gunman, but he never veered from his target. The sun was at his back, but it wouldn't be for long, and then the advantage he sought would be lost. Step upon step the drama that was to meet this town was unfolding, and there was nothing anybody in Dodge could do to stop it.

The badge on his gun belt was apparent. Most lawmen wore their shield on their shirt, but this fighter's bare chest seemed to be asking for lead, hiding behind nothing but the promise of a swift hand and a hair trigger. Ten paces from the town saloon he stopped and waited for the word to spread throughout the building he knew contained his "man." And then it happened. The towering figure of evil burst through the swinging doors of the bar and drew.

History does not speak well of what happened that day. Some witnesses say that not a shot was fired. Others claim that the deputy emptied his gun. What everybody does agree on is that they will never deputize another toddler. Most people say that the deputy just cried until his mother came and got him. Later that day the city council met to discuss what had gone wrong. It was such a big gun, such a shinny badge, and the two-year-old had one of the meanest stares in the county. Who could mock such authority?

The word "authority" implies one who is in control, one who knows or has power of some kind and, in general, the "truth." But when we talk about the "principle of authority," we must be clear that we are not talking about a person but a "power." Our example of the "baby authority" best juxtaposes these two concepts by recklessly trusting the oversight of the authority of the law to one who is incapable of the power of authority. This concept is unique to a study on deception because deception utilizes the concept of authority to manipulate people's perspective.

The deceptive principle of "authority" is not to be confused with an authority who deceives us. "Authority" when used as a verb, (not as a noun), assigns indiscriminate power to declare "what is" regardless of whether or not "what is" is true. The principle of authority usually appears uninvited into our lives when we either arrogantly or casually seek knowledge.

There is an old Chinese proverb that declares, "As there is no tiger on the mountain, the monkey becomes a king."[26] We could use this metaphor to remind ourselves that God must be the tiger on the mountain, or *we* may become the monkey. We may assign indiscriminate power to ourselves or others, power to decree what is and is not true regarding matters that we see dimly.

The Old Testament story of Israel demanding a king reminds us how easy it is to replace an established relationship with God. Better described perhaps as "misplaced authority," within this study "authority" is just another influence on our choices. The principle of authority becomes a principle of deception when authority is granted to someone or something other than that which is BEST. Not unlike pinning a sheriff's badge on a baby: one could create a deputy in a diaper, but is an infant really going to meet expectations? Did Israel's kings meet expectations?

The failure of Israel's kings was just another chapter in the long saga of God and Israel. God and His interaction with Israel seemed to be the major focus of the entire Old Testament. Approximately four thousand years of historical writings have documented Israel's declarations and celebrations of their God. Ask any self- respecting Jew during that time period, "Who is the authority in your life?" And they would answer, "The God of Abraham."

The early Jew would declare: "Of course God was Israel's God. Of course He was in charge; of course He knew best! Of course He had all power!" Yet we read in Numbers chapter two that all of those declarations actually delivered *faithlessness!* Faithlessness because we find Israel complaining to Moses about God Himself. Ignoring the obvious, they chose to believe that God wanted them to die in the desert. Here Israel's circumstances became "bigger than God." Although each one could "parrot" the expected answer, the reality is that God's authority shrunk as their circumstances grew. Time and time again God had to bring them back to reality. In this story we see that God chose to send snakes to bite them because of their murmuring against Him.

To remind them where their hope lay for salvation, in the authority of His being, God also provided a "snake bite cure." God had Moses form a brass snake and put it onto a pole. When the people looked upon the brass snake, they were healed. Ask again who the authority in their life was, and they would have probably answered (with one eye on you and one eye on the brass snake) "The God of Abraham." Yet hundreds of years later, the godly king, Hezekiah discovered a satanic surprise. Second Kings 18:4 says, "He (Hezekiah) removed the high places, smashed the sacred stones and cut down the Asherah poles. He broke into pieces the bronzed snake Moses had made, for up to that time the Israelites had been burning incense to it."

With a little time and deception, the bronze snake had become an authority. Although Israel could give the right answer to the question "Who is the authority in your life," the object of their faith was now a brass snake! It had gained considerable power over the people. God had again faded into the background of their reality, because they believed in what they could see—a hunk of metal, a brass authority.

Old Testament history repeats itself as the early Christian church finds that pseudo-authorities were a major problem for them as well. Jesus rebuked the Pharisees for putting the law in the position of authority as opposed to its rightful place as a "mirror," a standard that reveals our sin. Paul rebukes those who claimed to be followers of any specific teacher other then Jesus. Even post-apostolic history reeks of misplaced authority. For hundreds of years disputes on doctrinal issues were appealed to emperors (such as Constantine) who overstepped their authority. Eventually, the Middle Ages would record a number of church authorities placed in their positions by secular authorities.

These are just a few examples of how even well-intentioned people of God have historically found themselves submitting to the wrong things. This is the power of authority as an influence. It affects our lives when we recklessly abandon the leading of the Holy Spirit. The Holy Spirit and the "Word" will be our best protection from the danger of selecting a false authority. True authority is spiritual authority, which will be our leader in matters of spiritual warfare. Since Scripture warns that the weapons of our warfare are not carnal, we might need an authority that isn't carnal either.

Jeremiah (chapter 17) delivered his famous words "The heart is deceitful above all things" prefaced by this warning on authority: (17:5) "Thus saith the LORD; *Cursed be the man that trusteth in man,* and maketh flesh his arm, and whose heart departeth from the LORD. For he shall be like the heath in the desert, and shall not see when good cometh; but shall inhabit the parched places in the wilderness, in a salt land and not inhabited. The heart is deceitful above all things, and desperately wicked: who can know it?" (emphasis added).

We are armed with the very Spirit of God to help us choose the authority in our lives, but equivoque (the choice of no choice) will tend to limit our choices to a list created by our own desires. This is not unlike the unrestrained eater who asks himself "Do I want dark or milk chocolate today?" Carrots are never an option. Therefore, we set up dangerous criteria for accepting authorities into our lives. Our check list is riddled with our heart's selfish motives: Is he likable? Do I want what he's got? Can he help me achieve my goals? Do I already agree with him? The list goes on as we jump from one teaching to another seeking to have our ears "tickled" by the latest rising "star." These are dangerous options for choosing the boundaries of our lives, dangerous because deception never relents from manipulating our perspective and our desires. The reality is that the principle of authority (in our opening example it was the esoteric power of the law behind the badge) is often pinned onto the wrong people (the baby).

No doubt we obviously have many people to whom it is appropriate to submit a portion of our lives. The "trick" is submitting to Caesar only that which is Caesar's. As we come together to worship, we need to bring our own personal relationships into the assembly. We must not grant church leaders the authority to take responsibility for our own personal relationship with God. God will not absolve us of our responsibility to know Him.

But still we must submit to "fit." God is not the author of confusion. If we are not careful, we may chase off peace and order in "the body" when we promote ourselves to being "the authority" over an established hierarchy. There is a rightful and helpful place for authorities within the church structure. The Bible is clear on who qualifies as an authority and who does not. However, let us not forget that these authorities will not be ultimately responsible for your soul. This issue is between you and God, so be warned of false authorities allowed into your life by the principle of "authority."

Being a false authority is not always an indictment on the leader: many times the followers are to blame. They relinquish their personal obligations due to their own weaknesses or fears. Perhaps they are prey due to their own ignorance simply because they were too lazy to do the research. Left unchecked it will not be long before the false authority is setting, interpreting, and enforcing the "vision" as he (she) sees it, no matter how they happened to become "the authority."

The deceived may even find themselves dancing to the right tune, but for the wrong reasons. Unfortunately, once the flesh is in control, this principle of deception recognized as "authority" is firmly established over a real authority. When *an* authority gets in the way of *the* authority, it is a small step for followers to seek and mimic the visions of "monkey authorities." Unlike our deputy in a diaper, "monkey authorities" may not be so easily exposed. Perhaps one reason that there is a problem with the church in America today is that misplaced authority has contributed to it. Many of today's churches are operating on somebody else's vision because many of today's Christians are too!

It is easier to learn from a vision than be led by one, and it is safer to copy a vision than to receive an original one. Abraham was given an instruction by God to kill his son Isaac. Later on in the story, we learn that Abraham was given another word from God not to kill his son. It seems visions and words and instruction from God come from God in His way in His time. We need to have a relationship with God that gives us patience and ears to hear from God before we "kill" something we are not supposed to. We may inadvertently kill a pastor's ministry because we put him on a pedestal or we may kill our own personal vision before God can even reveal it to us.

It is fortunate for Isaac that his father was in constant communion with God and obeyed. What pain would have been added to this story had Job's friends been around to talk Abraham through his "sacrifice" dilemma? Through Abraham and Isaac, God has left a historical footnote that reminds us that the stakes can be high. For this reason, tuning in to the Holy Spirit is critical, because it is the central way God promises to lead us. Even the Bible requires God's revelation to be properly understood.

Misplaced authority is just one more weapon in Satan's arsenal of "principalities and powers." Eventually, we will find that our lives become testimonials to the wreckage a wrongfully empowered authority can inflict. The concept may be hard to identify at first. Most of us have had good authorities in our lives such as parents and teachers. But as the power of the parent's authority begins to wane, a child's peers may become his authority. Maybe the parents are replaced by a teacher, professor, or mentor. Mix a little time and apathy into the formula, and truth begins to migrate to perception as we seek knowledge. Our doctors may become our gods, our pastors become our idols, and our individual experiences make us our own experts on reality.

Allowing authorities into our lives is a major landmark in our human experience. Ultimately, the final authority in our lives will be selected on the basis of our faith. Wouldn't it have to be? How else can we know we have selected a good authority and a reliable standard? Didn't the early fathers of the church face this very issue? As late as the beginning of the third century, there was not church consensus on the authority of Scripture. Debates were common then, but the New Testament we have today is a product of a rooting out by reliable witnesses of the original words of Jesus. His teachings are the basis of our written author- ity, and we accept Jesus' teachings by faith. Faith is a gift, and each man (woman) has a measure of it. Faith grows by hearing the reliable words of Christ, confirmed by the witness of the Holy Spirit, and faith is abundantly available to those who seek after it. Faith is not a leap. Faith is a God-given step toward the realiza- tion of our hope, and it is proven by the evidence of the work of God within us.

Authority by deception "jumps" into the middle of that faith-building process and delivers an out-of-sequence answer to us. Soon there seems to be more direction and visions to choose from than we can decipher, and faith becomes a leap towards an apparent authority rather than a "walk" with a real one. We may grant to ourselves control, or we submit to attractive alternatives. Cults depend on these out-of-sequence leaps. They take Scripture or teachings out of context and "build" teachings that are unreliably "new." The credibility of our New Testament is the "in sequence" history established principles that the New Testament confirms, not invents. God's teachings are the same yesterday, today, and forever, void of leaps and new authorities.

"Leaping" is just a bad way to let one authority select another authority. Even when "leaping" starts from the right place and lands in the right place, it still misses the process of selecting a proper authority. Unfortunately, it happens far too often. Many children grow up with God as their authority simply because their *parents* said so. If at some time in our lives we do not abandon our parents' authority or the church's authority[27] and make God the object of our faith, we will miss the true authority. Choosing *the* authority in our lives should be a response to the "wooing" of the Holy Spirit and a prayer-filled experience rather than an accidental default to the path of least resistance.[28]

In God's wisdom (and yes even His mercy), He has utilized this fallen world to expose false authorities in our lives. Sometimes bad things happen to good people just to teach us that deception has caused our circumstances to dictate our authorities. Who are we to declare who is "good" enough to avoid bad circumstances? And by what authority do we have the right to declare anything God allows as a "bad" thing?

We see reflections of God's authority in His right to name His creation, and God declared His creation "good." As we see the ultimate authority (God) *grant* the right to name things to man (Adam), who is given dominion over the beasts on the earth, we find that man has seized the right to declare things "bad." Have we overstepped our authority? This "mark" of authority is consistent throughout history. Conquering Kings often renamed their conquered victims (Shadrach, Meshach, Abednego) to "mark" their property.[29] Even gods changed names as they moved from culture to culture.[30] Today in America, parents have the right to name their children, and a child who changes their name later on is usually struggling to break from their parents' authority. However, ultimate authority rests with the authority who can impose his will without assistance. God's mark of authority is obvious. No one is blind to God's mark (Romans 1:20), but some will have to die before they bow their knees and confess with their tongue that He is Lord.

Only God can declare what "is." Only a Creator has *earned* the right to control His creation. Was this not the lesson we learned from the story of Job? God gave Job (starting in chapter 38) a four-chapter discourse on true authority by asking Job, "Can you create this, can you do that, can you know this, can you make that, ...etc? Job learned that he had accepted the misplaced authority of his friends rather than God's authority. Realizing that he had been duped, Job ignores the council of his friends for God's council as he puts his hand over his mouth and listens to His Creator (Job 40:4).

True authority must have ultimate power to back its decrees or grant its authority to another backed by that same power. A mere king would need armies and cooperation. The pope needs a consensus of leaders to recognize him. Even a president with his finger "on the button" has no more power than the results of the consequences. It takes a King of kings to be the Lord of lords. Only mercy allows God's creation to discuss a choice of authorities and the fairness of our circumstances; wise people will grant Him that.

Many a Christian has missed or lost the truth of "God with us," the ultimate authority. It takes more than just prayer to "tap" into the internal voice of God that woos us. This relationship takes a preparation that presents our prayers with a humble and contrite heart. It comes through prayers of surrender and obedience to Him because He is our authority, both earned by God's ultimate power and granted by our free will. God is our authority, and we must settle for nothing less, no matter how attractive, no matter how easy, no matter how popular another authority may look. Authorities other than God can only offer limited power with some of the benefits.

CHAPTER SIX

Smack It With a Rock and See If It's Alive

Disguise

Polar bears eat seals. Seals seem to know this, and so they keep an ever watchful eye out for these dangerous predators. Nature has a way of allowing every creature a fair chance at survival, and the polar bear's white coat serves to balance the odds in this competition against the seal's keen eyes. However, polar bears do not just default to the use of their white coats, but seem to understand the principle of disguise. So adept are they at this principle that they have been filmed sneaking up on their prey while covering their black noses with their white paws.

Disguise is the principle whereby one thing we could readily identify is made to look like something else. In this case the polar bear cannot be identified by the seal because the bear is disguised as snow. The results of the bear's disguise may be fatal to even the most cautious seal.

The church is wearing a "disguise," and it is becoming increasingly more difficult to find the true church of God. Read any variety of the current popular books in any Christian bookstore, flip through a few of the religious programs on your television set, or attend different church services for a few weeks and then define the "Christian church." This is the perspective of the "world," and they cannot define, let alone understand, today's church. Since when has the Christian church ever been so popular, yet so hard, to find? To steal a line from the theme song of the *Midnight Cowboy*; "Everybody's talking at me, but I can't hear a word they're saying."

Now watch the day-to-day lives of those "believers" who make up the majority of the church and describe the power of God you see. What is it that attracts your attention? What stands out in the life of believers? Do you see love, joy, peace, long-suffering, gentleness...? How about unexplainable selfless sacrifices, victory, or the supernatural? In general, do Christians stand out or blend in? In your opinion has Christianity been relegated to a silent witness supporting a few "zealots" with an irritating voice in positions of influence, or is it a magnetic refuge of obvious truth?

Ultimate destruction caused by disguise has echoed its consequences for more than six thousand years. A beautiful angel took the form of a harmless creature and slithered into the history pages with the Fall of man. The Genesis account of Eve and the serpent sets a precedent for numerous other accounts recorded throughout the Bible that utilize the principle of disguise.

Judah's daughter-in-law disguised herself as a temple prostitute so as to have a son by Judah (Genesis 38).

Joshua was tricked into a covenant of protection with people he was sent to destroy when they disguised their identity and he failed to consult the Lord (Joshua 9).

Israel's first king, Saul, consulted a witch, betraying his own decree by disguising himself with the hopes of summoning the dead (1 Samuel 28).

Jeroboam's wife disguised herself to the prophet Ahijah so to get (hopefully good) information about her sick son. But God disclosed her trickery before she ever arrived to the prophet (1 Kings 14).

Israel's scout soldiers sent to Jericho were called spies, simply because they went disguised.[31] Isaac was deceived by his youngest son, who was disguised as his oldest son and was thus able to steal the family blessing. [32] And so it goes, deception after deception, marching through the pages of history, manipulating perspectives as part of an unrelenting human condition. Yes, deception is a *condition,* not a sin.

Some of the principles of deception, when taken as an individual component of life, do not necessarily equate to sin. But all of the principles of deception do equate to our need for help. First Corinthians 13:12 speaks of our human perspective: "For now we see through a glass, darkly; but then face to face: now I know in part; but then shall I know even as also I am known." In physical human history, deception will never cease, it will never be revealed soon enough, it will never give you a break, and it is never best.

For this reason we have trouble with accepting deception as anything but evil, because our limited understanding of deception tends to classify it as just "bad." But "bad" does not do deception justice, since deception can change from dark (lies) to light (placebos) so subtly. Meanwhile, deception is not just an earthly weapon; it is a spiritual condition—more powerful, more dangerous, and more common than sin. *More powerful* than sin because sin is the result of being deceived, not the force. *More dangerous* because deception cloaks our vulnerability to sin, and so we lose our fear of it. *More common* because deception does not always result in sin, but deception always accompanies it. Evil has not hidden the church from view, but deception has.

In his book *The Psychology of Deception,* author Jason Randal makes an important distinction between deception and persuasion.

He sugguests that a deceiver will present false or illegitimate evidence to influence, while a persuader will present the truth in a manner that the receiver of the information interprets to the persuader's advantage.[33] Here it becomes apparent that the motive may be sinful, but the deception may not be.

Women wear makeup and some color their hair. They harmlessly alter how others will perceive them by applying creams, powders, and colors to disguise features they want to hide or accentuate. This is deception by any definition; however,it does not violate the laws of God. Makeup is not bad. Sometimes it is good, but it is not "best." A perfect face and perfect complexion would be the best. A woman using makeup would not be labeled a "deceiver" until she denies its existence. God has made it clear that deception is not a random attack.[34] It is a part of life that we can look forward to shedding when we get to heaven, but for now we live with it. We as Christians need to shed a cloak of disguise that covers what we have to offer to the world. The "world" does not see us, but it thinks it does.

The world can only see our disguise, our façade. It only sees our results, for it cannot see our intents. Facts are negotiable. Perceptions are not. In other words, Christians need not bother to explain how loving, forgiving, and exciting they are to the "world." Even if it is true, it matters little if the "world" sees us otherwise. We need to realize that all of the facts of our faith cannot change the perception the world has of us. What the "unsaved" see is not always what is so, but in America it seems that what is seen is the only proof needed for believing in something.

It is human nature for us to believe that which we feel powerless to change.[35] Power-hungry egos are often disguised as statesmen and become our elected politicians. Abortion clinics are disguised as "health care" institutions, and we accept them. Our enemies are often disguised as friends. Pagan religious institutions are disguised as social clubs, and ethical social clubs are disguised as Christian institutions. In a world where there is every reason for cynicism, where suspicion is a virtue and vulnerability is rampant, how can we show the world Jesus?

Television has no problem showing the world Jesus. The popular cartoon *The Simpsons* is teaching the world all about Christianity. In an exposé on this show, one author wrote a book entitled *The Gospel According to the Simpsons*. The author hails the Simpsons as a good influence and a positive presentation regarding Christianity. Two writers claim to be Christians and insist that they can "pitch" blasphemous and sacrilegious jokes all day without it injuring their "personal spirits." But "The Gospel According to the Simpsons" is a Gospel defined by the struggle of good and evil. It promotes decent behavior and church attendance. It punishes those who do not acknowledge God and indorses the concept of an ultimate authority. In short, if virtual Christianity could save, this show would be a sermon. Perhaps *The Simpsons is* a great moral compass for a pagan society, but it has disguised true Christianity! It disguises "doing" as "being," and this show is subtly infiltrating the Gospel of Jesus Christ and Him crucified. How deceived do we have to be to laugh at blasphemous and sacrilegious jokes while bragging that they do not injure our "personal spirits" at all?

Too often we think we show the world Jesus by identifying and denouncing sin, but sin is not our biggest problem! Sin did not keep Jesus from meeting the woman at the well, or eating with Zaccheus, or healing the sick, or saving you. And sin does not hide God from the world. In fact, sin reveals the world's need for God. The authors submit that the world is looking for God, and sin is not impairing their vision. It's driving their quest! Satan knows that sin exposes our need for God, and since we can all agree that Satan is not going to renounce sin, it would follow Satan must try to "hide God." Who would guess that the Gospel of Christ could be so hidden that it is lost within "moral behavior"?

Hiding God means that Satan wants the world to see our faith disguised as just another option for serving ourselves. Our prayers to the world will sound like wishes, and our hope will be seen as mere determination. And can you blame the world? They see things wrong because their heart is deceitful above all things, and they cannot know it.

We can also blame ourselves. Deception is wreaking havoc with our testimonies without ever having to commit a single sin. Far too many of us have settled for a virtual Christian life. Could we defend our faith? The apostle Peter admonishes us to "sanctify the Lord God in your hearts: and be ready always to give an answer to every man that asketh you a reason of the hope that is in you with meekness and fear" (1 Peter 3:15).

Can we show the world the power of *answered* prayers that we claim to have access to? Does the world see a common theme of supernatural hope in all believers or just determination based on the individual's character?

If we are to "undisguise" the church, or should we say "unveil" it to the world, we must be identifiable, separate, and distinct. This does not mean "loud," "superior," or "weird." We must be real, obedient, and consistent at our own expense. These are impossible goals without the active power of God's Spirit motivating and leading believers. Without this spiritual help, we might tend to believe our own disguise.

We know that the world would choose Jesus, but we have goofed up. We have clothed ourselves in behavior for so long, we think we look good! The world wants true love, and true love does not just look good. It looks like Jesus! Regardless of what we as individuals or institutions say, no matter what we think, no matter what we believe, the world has rendered a verdict on us. Their perception is not flattering simply because deception has disguised the truth in so many different ways.

Prayer is sometimes disguised as religious behavior camouflaged in the forest of hope. Prayer should be talking to and hearing from God, but our words sometimes give us away. Listen to the way we tend to pray, and it sounds like we talk at God, not to Him. When we are talking to "real" people, we don't talk the same way as we do when we talk (at) God. "Bill, I really thank you for the present, Bill, and, Bill, I know you're listening to me right now, dear Bill, but, Bill I..."

Where does our hope lie to defeat this "dim mirror" syndrome? We need God more involved. We need to experience God personally, *then* shine to the world corporately. We are to be multiple witnesses, with many gifts each confirming the same message.

Perhaps this is why the psalmist invites us to "taste and see that the Lord is good" (Psalm 38:8). Beyond just taste, tasting involves the sense of touch (texture), the sense of smell, as well as being enhanced by our sense of sight. Information confirmed from multiple senses becomes much more trustworthy to us, but even more important is that personal, intimate experience leaves a lasting flavor of God's goodness in our memories. Once touched by God, all of our senses will lead us to conclude that the "Lord is good." Second Peter 1:16-21 informs us: "For we did not follow cunningly devised fables when we made known to you the power and coming of our Lord Jesus Christ, but were eyewitnesses of His majesty. For He received from God the Father honor and glory when such a voice came to Him from the Excellent Glory: 'This is My beloved Son, in whom I am well pleased.' And we heard this voice which came from heaven when we were with Him on the holy mountain. And so we have the prophetic word confirmed, which you do well to heed as a light that shines in a dark place, until the day dawns and the morning star rises in your hearts; knowing this first, that no prophecy of Scripture is of any private interpretation, for prophecy never came by the will of man, but holy men of God spoke as they were moved by the Holy Spirit." Peter teaches us that being an eyewitness, hearing God's voice, and having a word confirmed through the Holy Spirit all serve as multiple testimonies to truth.

This kind of relationship with God offers the world a distinct church. This is how the "world" begins to see our God. Only then can confirming biblical truths be seen in science, history, astronomy, archeology, and the testimonies of our own human experience. Consistent faith demonstrated with power and compassion wrapped in love, joy, peace, long-suffering, mercy, and self control is what the world needs to see. Anything less is going to be discarded by "outsiders" as just another philosophy disguised as "religion."[36]

How many paint jobs have sold a "lemon" car? How many new carpets have sold a moldy home? How many smiles have sold a relationship, and how many fables have sold a new religious belief? We live in a sophisticated America, and people do not want to be duped. Christians have been judged by many as just another needy people disguised as philosophers. In America today it's popular to be "spiritual," but it is not popular to be stupid. Christians need to demonstrate their claims, not just celebrate them on Sunday. If it is true that we are the only Jesus that the world will see, then thanks to us Jesus is disguised from the world too.

Has Christianity become a means to a lesser end? Could it be that worldly influence has become a disguise over the Christian life? Is it being packaged and sold as a lifestyle of receiving, when we were clearly created to be givers?[37] Disguise has been with us since the Fall, yet as the years pass by, we have continued to refine our ability to alter what we see with this deceptive principle.

Finally, this aspect of deception is important to understand because it shows the depth of just how little we can know about our human perspective while we are looking through a "dark glass." How can we know truth with so much influence available?

Are our desires God's, or does our heart deceive us? Does society implant those motivations inside of us, or is it a trick of Satan? With our choices controlled, our authorities confused, and bad things disguised as good things, we are left to wonder like Paul in Romans 7:24: "O wretched man that I am! who shall deliver me from the body of this death?" We live in "Babylon" subject to all the rules of this fallen world, and only the direction that has been God-given to us within the Shema, the work of Jesus at Calvary, the leading of the Holy Spirit, and our obedience can overcome the influences of this deception.

CHAPTER SEVEN

Lying Your Way
Through Trust

Suggestion

Eight sane people gained secret admission to twelve different hospitals located in five different states on the East and West coasts. The quality of the hospitals varied from old and shabby to quite new research-oriented and well-staffed ones. All but one was supported by federal, state, or university funds. One of the eight pseudopatients was a psychology student in his twenties. The other seven were older and 'established': three psychologists, a pediatrician, a psychiatrist, a painter, and a housewife. Except for alleging hallucinatory systems to gain admission and falsifying name, vocation, and employment to avoid identification, no other future alterations of person, history, or circumstances were made. Upon entering the psychiatric ward, each pseudopatient *'ceased simulating any systems of abnormality.'* (Rosenhan 1973:251) In spite of their show of sane behavior in the ward, in eleven of the twelve admissions, the experimenters were each diagnosed as 'schizophrenic.' In one admission that pseudopatient was diagnosed as 'manic depressive.' The perceptions of hospital staff, including psychiatrist, were so controlled by the psychiatric setting and by what they expected that they failed to differentiate any of the pseudopatients from the real patients" (Rosenhan 1973:250-258:cited from Hsu1983:426)[38]

The above story is true and might easily be dismissed as just another "can't see the forest for the trees" antidote, but it actually introduces a totally different problem affecting our Christian lives today. Here we see the tendency of even the "experts" to be led by the deception of suggestion. But professionals are not the only people duped by the power of suggestion. All of us live under a "cloud" of suggestion that continues to be propagated by our culture, our desires, and specifically our faith via our perspective of "orthodoxy." Take for instance the typical twentieth-century American idea of a wedding, a bride, or a wedding feast and compare them to the culture of the biblical authors. It doesn't take long to see that the celebrations that they used as metaphors do not translate to us as they did to the early church, nor do they even translate to other cultures of our days!

In his historical accounts of what the early church looked like, Dr. Justo Gonzalez (the youngest person ever awarded a Ph.D in historical theology at Yale) gives a rapid-fire account of some of the differences: The early church did not have pastors (p. 97.) They met on Sundays specifically to eat a meal and celebrated communion in a joyous way, not a somber mood (p. 94.) They did not believe teaching to be the central event when they met. (p. 94) Churches only allowed the baptized to attend their services (p. 94) Baptisms were once a year and it was to be done in "living" (running) water, after which they were anointed with oil and welcomed into the royal priesthood (p. 96) "Evangelism did not take place in the churches, but as Celsus said, in kitchens, shops, and markets." (p. 99)[39]

Can you imagine a "noisy" communion service, or not focusing on the pastor's ability to teach, or asking attendees for their "credentials" in church today? The point here is that the way things are now *suggests* to us that we can ignore the way things were, and this is fatal for our ability to know the way things should be!

Our specific experience and culture are subtly influencing how we perceive things should be. The deceptive principle of suggestion is validating relatively young "orthodoxy" and allowing "necessary" change. It may be some of this is acceptable, but have we come to be a group of believers who "believe" the church should use its "position" to take the "lead" in our evolving understanding of "church"?

The church as an institution is an evolving thing. Look how the early church has now evolved to be the overseer of evangelism, or how it now takes the lead for our personal instruction in the faith, how it specializes in counseling on life's problems, or, for that matter, how we insist it give us our "daily bread." Compare our idea of "the faith" to Gonzalez's conclusion to his chapter on the early Christian church: "In conclusion, the ancient Christian church was composed mostly of humble folk for whom the fact of having been adopted as heirs of the King of Kings was a source of great joy. This was expressed in the joy of their worship, in their art, in their life together and in their valiant deaths. The daily life of most of these Christians took place in the drab routine in which the poor in all societies must live. But they rejoiced in the hope of a new light that would destroy the dark injustice and idolatry of their society." (p. 101) We would like to think this describes the church today, but does it?

Suggestion is a principle of deception that contributes to the decline of truth in our lives and, therefore, in our church. The above examples are only a few of hundreds the authors could have cited. False beliefs are made possible, because to a deceiver, a lie is as good as the truth if you can get somebody to believe it.

However, a single false *suggestion* can be even more powerful than many lies. Body language, voice inflections, casual glances, and general appearances all work just fine to deceive.

There is a very old "magic" trick that utilizes suggestion and leads the audience to believe that the sneaky performer can read minds. To accomplish this he has one member of the audience write anything they want onto a paper he cannot see. The paper is torn up and burned, after which, that which was written down on the paper is "divined" by the magician. The interesting thing about this particular effect is that with the aid of suggestion, what could have been looked upon as a simple stunt becomes an impossible miracle.

You see, the performer does not actually get the message right; instead he "misses" the message just enough to apologize for failing, but close enough to have the audience praise his amazing closeness. For instance, had the audience member written "RED," then the performer (yes, he has a method of secretly reading it) may fumble around a bit and "see" a rose or blood. "No, no, you wrote a word, a small word...I see an apple, no a rose? I'm so sorry. I can't seem to picture in my mind what you wrote. I'll say rose, but I don't think the word has any *O*'s in it. What *did* you write? Although the magician knew the word, if he had been exactly right, the audience could suspect he peeked (which he did). But because he "missed," the *suggestion* is that he did not peek or he would have gotten it exactly right.

Years of performing has taught professional deceivers that suggestion is a powerful way to make believers believe for themselves. This trick features the audience rejecting the performer's apology in lieu of their praises for being an obvious "seer," and who cares if he was not 100 percent right? He was close enough! This trick wins over even the most skeptical of audiences, because the power of suggestion allows "close enough" to be the same thing as "accurate."

Present this deceptive concoction of suggestion to a person who is willing or even wanting to believe, and you get a "form" of the truth. Not the truth that is owned by reality, but "truth" that is owned by one's belief. Making this same point, C.S. Lewis seems to mock himself for "feeling" safer in high seas in a small boat than he does secure on land gazing over a steep cliff.[40] Suggestion lies!

Elijah ran from Jezebel's threat of death in self-pity, believing that he was all alone in his faith. After being a part of one of the most mighty examples of God's power and one of the most impressive displays of faith in Scripture, who would have guessed that Elijah would become so discouraged that he would want to die (1 Kings 19)?

The answer is simple, Elijah did not see things as God saw them; Elijah was deceived. Was he confused? No, he was not confused. He knew what he wanted. Was he misdirected? No, he was not misdirected. He was actually waiting for direction. Was Elijah a victim of a ruse, or was something disguised? No! Elijah was a victim of his feelings, his emotions, his intellect, and his limited powers of observation. "You will die," says Jezebel; "You're all alone," says his heart; "You are tired," says his mind, and so the power of suggestion transformed Elijah's incredible victories into bad memories.

God does not forsake the righteous nor leave Elijah begging for bread. He comes to Elijah's rescue. God relieves Elijah of his commission and anoints Elisha to carry on. Elijah is being prepared to go home. He will not get another lesson in faith. He will not spend years learning about the power of God. Elijah gets a well-deserved rest from the constant faith-draining deception called "suggestion." No more rumors, no more threats, no more guessing, no more lies.[41]

Maintaining our deceptions has become a way of life for us. If we believe something, our first impulse is to defend it, and yet how many of the basics of our faith could we defend against an intelligent inquirer? If popular radio talk shows in Seattle are any example, then very few could. Misinformation, poor exegesis, hearsay, and personal experiences mix up a batch of Christian doctrine with Scripture to deliver weak testimonies of many a sincere Christian. The truth is that our western twentieth-century perspective suggests that we Americans have a lock on accuracy, yet Gonzalez (p. 97) points out that "as the church became increasingly Gentile, the danger of heresies was greater." Although Gonzalez does not say why, we can: deception, deception called cultural influence via "suggestion." Americans do not always seek the truth. We often seek data from a limited environment that agrees with our beliefs and promotes our existing lifestyle.[42] To our own peril, our opinions become facts.

The church in America today is not unique. Our hospitals, our government, our educational system, and even our scientists have fallen victim to the principle of "suggestion." It seems to be an American institution!

Even beyond trying to find evidence to support our predisposed beliefs, we tend to get most of our information from observations. This is not a good way to learn about or practice our faith. Imagine learning how to drive only from watching our friends. How can one learn the actual requirements of the law when your psuedo-driving instructor does not do everything the law requires? It would seem to you that their ways are acceptable, therefore legal and duplicable. Then you would teach your children how to drive as you learned to drive, with the additional benefit of trial and error, wrecks and tickets.

Then what if we learned to worship only by watching our friends at church?[43] What if we learned God's will for our lives only by attending seventeen years of Sunday morning sermons? What if we learned about the power of God only from observing the *results* of our own self-serving prayers? What if we learned to give simply by assessing the minimum we seemed to get away with? What if we learned to treat others only by how we were treated? What if a "decent" missionary support offering only needed to equal last year's giving? What if tradition was more important than truth?

Herein lies the power of suggestion. The way things *are* suggests that this is the way things *should be*. The status quo is what we strive for. Minimum standards replace the possibilities offered to us in Scripture. The best examples of godly people become our mentors to mimic, even though we haven't the remotest concept of their private lives. Let's face it, when it comes to grading our personal relationship with Christ, we grade on a curve. We look at the pew next to us and we compare.

Logic suggests that observing cause and effect can organize our community standards into a scientific formula of acceptable behavior. It is a good thing for Elijah that he did not take the scientific approach for gathering data. Elijah did not seek out some positive aspects of a pagan life that he could tolerate so that he could live among the heathen with a clear conscience and a compromised God. Instead, he sought truth: turning towards Jehovah God, he found truth and was given total deliverance and relief.

The power of suggestion may bring relief, but it will only be enjoyed for a short time, because it is deception. It deceives people into living on lies built on unsupported facts, feelings, and then ultimately beliefs. It creates its own reality and will eventually invite folks to recklessly discard Elijah's truth while substituting it with the pathetic declaration, "Look at me, I'm a Christian."

Looking back to the true story of the eight fake patients diagnosed as mentally ill, we can see that not everybody who is enrolled in a hospital should be there. We also learned that the professionals helping those "patients" featured some major problems with their perspective. This story reminds us that we do not see things as *they* are, but we see things as *we* are.

It has always been true of human nature. We should not mistake our own perspective for reality. When Moses got his report back from the "men of every tribe" sent to spy out the land of Canaan, most of the men reported that the land was not obtainable. The people there were too big and strong. In fact, Numbers 13:33 tells us that the *"children of Israel saw themselves as insects."* Isn't it interesting that not long after entering the land promised, Rahab the harlot informs these same people, saying: " I know that the LORD hath given you the land, and that your terror is fallen upon us, *and that all the inhabitants of the land faint because of you"* (Joshua 2:9 emphasis added).

There you have it. Israel saw themselves as "insects," while their enemies saw Israel as invincable. Classic false belief because fear suggested that the goal was not worth the cost. Truly we do see things the way *we* are. It's called perspective, and 1 Corinthians 13:12 says ours is pretty dim.

CHAPTER EIGHT

Three Eyes
Follow the Pea

Confusion

My Dear Wormwood,

"I note what you say about guiding your patient's reading and taking care that he sees a good deal of his materialist friend. But are you not being a trifle naif? It sounds as if you suppose that argument was the way to keep him out of the Enemy's clutches. That might have been so if he had lived a few centuries earlier. At that time humans still knew pretty well when a thing was proved and when it was not; and when it was proved they really believed it. They still connected thinking with doing and were prepared to alter their way of life as a result of a chain of reasoning. But what with the daily press, radio, television and other such weapons we have largely altered that. Your man has been accustomed ever since he was a boy, to a dozen incompatible philosophies dancing about together inside his head. He doesn't think about doctrines as primarily 'true' or 'false,' but as 'academic' or 'practical,' 'outworn' or 'contemporary,' 'conventional' or 'ruthless.' Jargon, not argument, is your best ally in keeping him from the Church."[44]

These were the first words C.S. Lewis had his deceptive demon Screwtape write to his apprentice demon and nephew, Wormwood. An idea that had spawned in Lewis's head back in 1940 eventually became known as *The Screwtape Letters* and would emerge as the most famous exposé on demons ever printed. Who can read *The Screwtape Letters* and not personally relate to the common themes exposed? This fascinating novel unveils Lewis's idea regarding the thinking of demons and the application of deception. Lewis also lays the best possible foundation that these authors could wish for our own thesis.

Every principle of deception is utilized by Lewis's demons, but the principles lie unnoticed beneath the subversive manipulation of the victim. In every one of the Screwtape letters, Uncle Screwtape identifies weaknesses in the human condition and plans his advantage. Consistently, Wormwood is directed to influence the victim by unidentified means as he is told to "guide," "hide," "change," "distract," etc. As one reads the "tricks" of Satan, what is not apparent is HOW he "guides," "hides," "changes," "distracts," etc.

In the above quote, Screwtape has correctly implied that "confusion" is a viable weapon against us when he states: "Your man has been accustomed ever since he was a boy, to a dozen incompatible philosophies dancing about together inside his head. He doesn't think about doctrines as primarily 'true' or 'false,' but as 'academic' or 'practical,' 'outworn' or 'contemporary,' 'conventional' or 'ruthless.' Jargon, not argument, is your best ally in keeping him from the Church."

We are about to explore the principle of deception known as confusion, and we agree with Lewis that it is Satan's best ally in keeping us from becoming the "true church." Confusion is different from all of the other principles of deception because confusion is not only a principle of deception; it is a result of deception. Therefore, confusion not only messes with our "journey"; it may also define our destination: We wind up barely a Christian with just some of the benefits.

Confusion may be the most common identifiable principle of deception that we encounter every day of our lives. We can actually feel confused because it often inflicts emotional stress on us. Too much information, too little information, distractions, advice, doctrines, dogma, opinions, desires. We have new sources springing up every day: new books, television programs, new products, new studies, new leaders, new experts. Add to our growing "bank" of individual experiences the constant unveiling of "Gods latest revelations," and we become overwhelmed with the "jargon" of confusion.

Confusion affects the victim's senses, the victim's memory, the victim's desires, and the victim's choices.[45] Not one of these targets is left in better condition after they meet the deception of confusion. Depression, helplessness, loss of focus, no direction, arguments, misinterpreted experiences, all leave the victim of confusion vulnerable to questionable outside influences. C.S. Lewis was able to tell this same truth in a delightful compilation of letters designed to reveal the *power* of demonic warfare. It is our contention that understanding the *principles* of deception helps us better understand the rules of engagement regarding demonic warfare.

Our battle with Satan will not always play out with a happy ending as it did in Lewis's book. Nor is it possible to list all the ways confusion might fight us. This is why the battle against Satan would be easier to fight if it was a fight against flesh and blood. At least we could see what we are up against. But we do not battle against flesh and blood, but we battle against principalities and powers that confuse our understanding of how the enemy works. Satan gets blamed too often for the thoughts we are not proud of, emotions that reveal our weaknesses, or sin that *originates* in our lives.

Demon possession aside, Satan's only control over our thoughts, emotions, or our sin are the principles of deception. Scientific, time-tested, provable, and repeatable principles that become the process whereby sin gains its power. Satan does not cast a "spell" that God must counteract. He does not have a special potion that creates lusts, arrogance, ignorance, slothfulness, and other sins and vulnerabilities. Our enemy cannot inflict these traits on us until we open ourselves to them. To paraphrase Dariel Fitzkee in his deception thesis entitled "Magic by Misdirection": "The deceiver exercises absolute control over his victim, by controlling the victim's attention. The deceiver forestalls it by catching it relaxed, by dulling it, scattering it, diverting it, distracting it and openly moving it away, He cleverly, skillfully mixes the true with the false...and all is built on an unshakable foundation of naturalness, plausibility and conviction."[46] We contend that our own "born into" sinful nature (our heart) is a powerful deceiver that generates this same method of control over our attention, then we choose to sin. Once this kind of influence has "deceived" us, the power of sin begins other predictable consequences.

Professional magicians (the professional magicians we are talking about here are just entertainers and have no real *majik* powers) study the principles of deception for two reasons. First, they know these principles are critical for scientific reliability in fooling an audience with new *tricks*.[47] Secondly, if one is a knowledgeable deceiver, then *tricks* can be tailored to the vulnerability of the audience. (An effect may look exactly the same on TV as it did at your child's birthday party, but the method often needs to be quite different.) Empowered with this knowledge, new combinations of deceptions can be concocted to create a labyrinth of confusion seemingly without solution. Like Uncle Screwtape, magicians know that confusing people always helps to deceive them. It plays to the limitations of their senses, and it comes in many different forms.

Confusion can aid the cheating husband in covering the smell of perfume simply by smoking a cigar on his drive home, as the strong smell covers the weak. Confusion allows the dentist to push the needle into your gum with less sensation of pain because as he quickly wiggles your lip, your mind is confused by the different sensory inputs. Confusion of a person's senses is easy to demonstrate. The carney con man utilizes a tiny pea and three shells on the top of a small table. After covering the pea with one of the shells, he begins to move the three shells around the table top in a high-speed manner. The con man (knowing the limitations of the human brain) can move the pea from shell to shell undetected. He has been trained to know that the large movement (moving the shells) covers the small movement (rolling the peas out the back of the shell). Here, an adept deceiver proves that confusion can have its way with our brain's limitations.

Everyone with a brain is a candidate for confusion. We only possess the ability to concern ourselves with a limited number of priorities, so this principle just waits. While other principles of deception might misdirect, hide, present, or change our priorities, confusion will eventually own our priorities. It is almost impossible to substantially prioritize our time or our actions when we are confused by our circumstances. Mature Christians are trained to pray through their confused state, but the unsaved are seldom "confused" into God's family.

As Uncle Screwtape pointed out in his first letter, confusion does not have to present a case against God: "Jargon, not argument, is your best ally in keeping him from the Church." Random or conflicting ideas (Jargon) are all that Satan needs to turn the unsaved "off" when it comes to Christianity. Curiosity may motivate the world into asking us, "Is Christianity institutional or individual?" "Is salvation by works or belief?" But based on the assorted answers they hear, what makes us think that the world would ever care to distinguish between our dogma, doctrines, and opinions?

Confusion does not distinguish anything for anyone. This principality is empowered by the concept that only the most obvious need or urgent situation will get our immediate attention. Confusion does not keep us from acting on information. It just severely hinders us from acting on information correctly. With confusion in our lives we have trouble processing logical steps to clarity. If at some point some type of clarity does not emerge for us, we will tend to panic.

Magicians who choose to routine an act utilizing the principle of confusion must be careful not to frustrate their audience. Too much confusion can render one's senses hopelessly inadequate. For maximum impact, confusion must be applied subtly enough to be tolerated. Therefore, a well-trained deceiver must make confusion tolerable, and the best confusion will even provoke the victim's own desires.

A pickpocket routine performed for entertainment in a theater is a great study in subtle confusion. It is one thing to sneak up behind somebody in a crowded mall and take the wallet out of their back pocket. It is a totally different challenge to stealthily pick the pockets of an audience member who *knows* that you are a pickpocket. Misdirection is usually a pickpocket's greatest weapon, but without the element of surprise, he must resort to confusion.[48]

Confusing his "on stage" victim's desires becomes his objective. The pickpocket knows that before the show begins, probably the reason that his "target" bought a ticket to a pickpocket show is the desire to catch him picking pockets and to see how it is done. The performer must bombard his selected "victim" with multiple desires, confusing the desire to catch him with many other desires. Other desires such as: "I don't want to be laughed at, I don't want to be made a fool, I don't want to be embarrassed, I don't want to look stupid, I want to look good, I want to be cool, etc." The entertainer does not want his "victim" relaxed. By keeping the target laughing, worried, moving, talking, and ultimately chasing implanted desires, the deceiver achieves his goal.[49]

In this same manner, valuable direction for our own lives may become just as confused. Self-serving opinions, impulsive desires, too many authorities, and random goals prove Proverbs 29:18: "Where there is no vision, the people are scattered." Ask yourself, "Do I want to evangelize the lost or just concentrate on staying saved myself?" "Do I want to impact my community or have it impact me?" "Do I want to invite the world to 'see my faith' or do I just want to tell them about it?" Confusion will have us answering these kinds of questions differently, depending on our mood, our circumstances, or our whims. Furthermore, confusion brings lost visions together. Here, it is common to find religious programs that just maintain themselves. Confusion is the catalyst for new denominations that have no real theological differences. Finally, confusion "buries" any hope of a specific vision for us, allowing only a stab at the "success" formulas concocted by the mega-churches. Confusion almost seems attracted to a lost vision, and it will eventually produce a scattered people.

Six thousand years ago, a people handpicked by God started a trek to a promised land of blessing. Is it any surprise that Satan would landscape the trail with confusion? As Israel conquered its enemies, Israel acquired cultures and beliefs that seemed to be attractive. Multiple influences, more opportunity, lots of distractions and pagan beliefs offered too many choices to be ignored. Failing to obey the command of God, memories began to fade. Confused by the possibilities that they saw as options, the Old Testament reveals that Israel's history is a history of forgetting their first love. Satan had "picked their pockets," not in a crowded mall, but from right under the hand of God!

The story of Israel's moral failure proves once again that confusion does not mean that random events or ideas cannot be predicted. As we already stated earlier, deception and all of its principles are repeatable, observable, and predictable. This includes confusion. Acts chapter 19 tells of an incident that happened over nineteen hundred years ago in Ephesus with repeatable, observable, and predictable results.

A silversmith named Demetrius heard that the Christians were teaching that the gods he was casting in silver really were not gods at all. Threatened with less income, this man incited people in the same trade as him to unite. It was not long before the yelling and protesting and chanting had spread throughout the city. Verse 32 reveals that the noise and emotions were so high that the people were confused: so confused, it says, that many did not even know why they were there.

It is believed that the laws in Ephesus at the time demanded the death penalty for anyone who incited or participated in a riot.[50] (When the town clerk pointed out this fact the crowd dispersed.) Three predictable concepts consistently arise around the principle of confusion, and they are all contained within this biblical account of confusion.

First, confusion spreads. It seems to be contagious when it is allowed to operate among people. But confusion also spreads within our lives even if we are the only ones involved. It starts out with questions, involves too many answers, impacts one emotion after another, and soon becomes unsolvable without help.

The next effect confusion always seems to have is that it causes people to lose their purpose. In the Bible story related above, many people did not even know why they were involved. Likewise, people lost their purpose in the building of the tower of Babel when their language was confused, and Job was tempted to lose sight of his place before God, thanks to many of his friends' advice. Gideon's army attacked the Midianites with lanterns and pots and pans in the middle of the night. Apparently, sheer confusion sent the enemy running, and they fought so ineffectively that three hundred of Gideon's men defeated the scattered Midianite army.

Finally, confusion always creates an opening for a leader. Confused people are vulnerable and usually willing to listen to an obvious or clear direction that can end the constant tug of war between emotions and perception. A myriad of answers seem to follow confusion. The answers need not be true. They only have to sound reasonable and satisfying. Whoever gets there first with an answer will probably win an audience.

Magicians understand the void created by confusion, and they are skillfully trained to fill that void with anything that serves their purpose. That is why "It's up my sleeve" and "I did it with mirrors" have been deceptively offered to explain everything. False answers for confused people have unlimited possibilities. Magicians thrive on confused people, as do dictators, cults, some divorce attorneys or politicians, and Satan.

Confusion leaves lasting marks. The symptoms of confusion are never actually hidden from us, but confusion is all but invisible to our recall. Confusion leaves its residue within a person's memory. This is provable on any given day, on any given stage: One of the simplest card tricks to perform involves displaying and then inserting the two of hearts and three of diamonds into a deck of cards that has previously been set up with just the opposite cards; the two of diamonds and three of hearts on the top of it. Once the first two cards are lost into the deck, the second two cards are produced from the top of the deck. Nobody notices that the cards are exact opposites of each other. Our memories tend to remember just "red twos and red threes."

It is not just card tricks that expose our vulnerability to confused memories. Life is not much kinder to our minds either. Confusion allows us to recall what we perceived and stored, and not necessarily what we saw. We all know and could cite our own personal stories of false memories. But even the police know and fear the failure of their recollections. Training against poor perceptions of their experiences, instructors display photos of suspects and then have officers recite what they saw. Many times the officers saw and remembered wrong.[51]

Have Christians seen correctly but remembered wrong? We contend that this is deception's first attack on our new life in Christ. Confusion began its work on us the day the Holy Spirit gave us our chance to see things clearly. We clearly saw our condition, clearly saw our only salvation in the sacrifice of Jesus. Until confusion began its work on us, we saw ultimate hope and felt ultimate love. There was a time we had a fresh realization. We understood that we had grieved God, we saw our separation from God because of our sin, we saw sin kill Jesus, and we mourned.

Although we still know about sin and we still believe sin is to be avoided, the "edge" is gone. It is not the years that have taken the "edge" off of our perspective of sin. We may blame "time" and the fact that all of our experiences eventually fade in intensity. But actually we can thank the principle of confusion for affecting our ability to mourn our sin.

There is probably more mourning in the prisons and hospitals and homeless shelters across America today than in our churches. More mourning in these places simply because we mourn our pain. But mourning over sin because it hurt us is not the same as mourning over sin because it grieves God. A meaningful relationship with God requires that we know the difference, so confusion even attacks our repentance!

Struggling against sin, hiding sin, regretting sin, avoiding sin, repenting and confessing have offered so many things to "do" with our sin that confusion finds opportunity here. Confused, our focus is drawn away from the realization of sin's original grip: now we hate sin, but we used to mourn over it. We lose some of the impact and beauty of our salvation because we have lost sight of our original selves, and thanks to confusion we have even missed the symptoms.

Confusion is a powerful influence when we do not recognize its symptoms. The wisdom we gain from order, focus, and clarity may not be consciously missed when they are missing from our lives. Confusion robs us of order, focus, and clarity, and whether we know it or not, we miss out on a lot more than just peace when confusion comes around. Peace is the enemy of confusion and vice versa. James 3:16-17 warns us that "for where envying and strife is, there is confusion and every evil work. But the wisdom that is from above is first pure, then peaceable, gentle, and easy to be intreated, full of mercy and good fruits, without partiality, and without hypocrisy."

Satan knows that we would be undefeatable witnesses for Christ if we were first pure, then peaceable, gentle, and easy to be intreated, full of mercy and good fruits, without partiality, and without hypocrisy. Therefore, with a little help from our ignorance and confused by our lack of vision, Satan offers to define our mission to the world. "The world does not know that you exist," he says. "Take your standards and promote them, learn your liturgy and profess tradition, wave your Bible and 'thump' it." Honestly believing that we are the poster children for order, focus, and clarity, off we go to "do," while all of the time forgetting that we were called to "be." Thanks to confusion, for all of our pointing and talking and directing, the world still misses truth.

Perhaps a good example of this tendency for Christians to "direct traffic" can be seen in how a magical entertainer will use a "magic" wand. Claiming that his ability to perform tricks is contained within the wand itself, he focuses attention onto a single black-and-white stick that moves your attention from place to place. This "pointer" seems to bring focus and better clarity as to where to direct your attention. In reality, it adds another element to misdirection. This simple tool compounds the confusion that is actually taking place: in addition to the performer, the props and assistants, the wand has become just another object for your eyes to follow.

Unfortunately, many Christians have unwittingly become a "wand" instead of a witness. Placed smack-dab in the middle of a country that needs to see Jesus, many of us are more comfortable orchestrating the "game plan" than living it out. We tend to confuse our mission with elaborate church presentations or doctrinal proclamations. We point towards Christ with a list of acceptable behaviors tied to the promise of an eternal reward. But our personal witness seldom seems to emerge obvious from our relationship with God. Confused, the world does not see a God of love who invites us to "be" a part of His eternity.

Confusion almost seems to reign as king on earth. So rampant is confusion, who of us has not at one time complained that "I just can't hear God's voice"? We have lost our "ears to hear" somewhere along the path of life. Our confused memories, our confused senses, and our confused understandings tend to confuse our goals. Confused goals lead to confused efforts, not to mention confused prayers. Confusion, according to Uncle Screwtape in his twenty-fourth letter to his demon nephew, is a *good thing*. This same letter reveals that C.S. Lewis understood; when all else fails, the advice from Hell that says, "Success depends on confusion."[52] We do not want to be Satan's victims as he hides the truth from us. Confusion must not reign supreme! Hopefully, in spite of the world's distractions, we can still hear Jesus' declaration better than Pilate did when he asked Jesus: "Are you a king then? Jesus answered, You say that I am a king. To this end was I born, and for this cause I came into the world, that I should bear witness to the truth. Every one that is on the side of truth hears my voice" (John 18:37).

CHAPTER NINE

No Wine Before Its Time

Anticipation

God did not do what He was supposed to do. Ask the rabbis of Jesus' day, and they will tell you God will not come as a baby, God will not die on a cross, and God will not accept unclean Gentiles. Actually, God is full of surprises, and if we listen He will inform us of His ways. His ways are not our ways, but the next principle of deception, known as the principle of anticipation, has little use for instruction.

Christians believe that the first-century Jews missed the truth because they did not rightly interpret prophecy, because they were stubborn, because they were blind, and because they assumed that God would do things differently. Christians today would be well advised to take heed of the mistakes of the first-century Jew regarding what we think God will do in our futures.

When I was a kid (T.J.), an elderly woman in our church claimed to have heard from God and announced to the congregation that Jesus was coming back before her life was over. The pastor graciously smiled and, winking, told her that he would not preach that as gospel. "However," he said, "God will come back before 1988 because that will be the end of one generation since the restoration of Israel, and that is God's promise." Did God break a promise, or did a great, well-meaning pastor assume too much?

How about it, are we really reading the book of Revelation in today's newspapers as some teachers claim? Many believe John's revelation is our future. Somewhere, somehow, hidden beneath the mystery of the "seals and plagues and beasts and trumpets," the end of the story is contained. And what an amazing story it is! *In order to please Himself, an inconceivable God creates a finite microcosm of forever and places beings made "after his image" into this environment knowing that they would fail. Being consistent to His own nature, this Creator expresses love by becoming a created being and dying to satisfy His own requirement for justice, thereby offering to inhabit the very lives He intends to save and proclaiming the right in that creation's eyes to judge the souls of those who reject Him.*[53]

One cannot help but ask oneself: really, why, how, when? Not unlike the historical Jews, Christians anticipate the return of God to earth to establish His reign with us at His side while systematically avenging us in respect to our adversaries. Some believe that the book of Revelation introduces us to the horror, the dangers, the spiritual happenings, and the end of the world as we know it. This book wraps up the story by warning us that preparation is the only hope we have, so be ready and watch, do not be deceived, the end is near. This amazing reality, believed by many Christians as the ultimate reality, is assumed to be "working in their favor." Christians read the end of the story and assume that this is their story of victory, their ultimate time to "win." This is exactly what the first-century Jew believed. But they were wrong, and we are right, right?

The book of Revelation allows for interpretations ranging from an "amillennial[54] view to a preterist[55] view to a premillennial[56] or postmillennial[57] view." Whatever you may believe this book is meant to tell us, the fact remains that the author was shown it in a vision and then *instructed to hide it*.[58] At least a portion of this book has *yet to come to pass,* and historically any *attempt to interpret it perfectly has failed.*[59] But humans tend to seek out men and women who promise to interpret the symbols in Revelation according to the daily newspaper usually from a middle-class, twentieth-century, western perspective. This allows an entry point for the principle of deception known as anticipation. Taking advantage of our curiosity, impatience, and gullibility, its unbalanced interest towards earthly events has created divisions and discouraged those who have unfulfilled assumptions. This type of anticipation becomes a dangerous distraction from Christ's Great Commission—to make disciples.

By definition anticipation has the victim assume too much. When we assume too much in our prayer life or expectations of others, anticipation can weaken our faith. We are told to live by faith, not assumption. It is important to get this right because assumption will fail us, and faith will not. Expecting a miracle is not necessarily the same thing as believing God heard and is in control. Having God respond to our prayers in our requested manner is an unpredictable blessing. If we love God and are called according to His purpose, we can have faith that all things will work together for our good, but we cannot anticipate God's timing, method, or lesson. Perhaps some quiet time in prayer will reveal His agenda through the Spirit, but short of a word of knowledge, only time will correct our assumptions.

Many people assume that when I (B.L.) give a word of knowledge over somebody's life it will automatically happen. Actually, I have heard hundreds of reports over the years of amazing events and fulfillments of words of knowledge, but it isn't always so. Words of knowledge are words from God that speak direction and encouragement into a person's life when they choose to live by faith. It is trusting God or obeying Him that will see the events delivered as promised. We should not assume God spoke to us for the sake of just knowledge, He speaks to initiate action, and action requires faith.

If we could *always* receive a known outcome from a *persistent* desire, then assumption would be validated and sincerity would be our god. But much of life is unpredictable; a predictable effect does not always follow the cause. Good things do not always happen to good people. Water exposed to 32 degrees Fahrenheit does not always produce the same snowflake. Science cannot explain the diversity of life. It cannot repair the wounds of the heart, and prayer is not a formula.

If we are not careful we will only embarrass ourselves by anticipating God's reaction to our petitions. Many believers insist that "God will answer your prayers for healing, prayers to pay off debt, prayers for restored marriages," and the list goes on and on. The world is assured that for Christians, God's answers are "Yea and amen!" Is this faith, or is it deceptive anticipation? What happens when in spite of your prayers the loved one you prayed for dies, you are forced into bankruptcy, or your wife leaves you?

Your response will answer the question: "Was it assumption or faith?" Do you stand silent, waiting to hear God to show you what you missed? Can you bring yourself to regroup your faith and learn to seek God's will and pray wiser? If so, good, for we are all still learning about walking in faith.

On the other hand, if you *always* assume that sin or lack of faith was the problem, or you *always* just shrug off unanswered prayer as "God's will," then you might consider paying some attention to this deception. Because if it was not something else, our unanswered prayers can only be attributed to the fact that we were presumptuous. We assumed something and we assumed wrong. We thought we knew but we didn't. This is discrediting us as Christians, and it is confusing the world about God.

Whatever it is that you believe about prayer, prayer is talking to God. You and Him. Could it be that we have forgotten that all the things we pray and ask God to do *for* us may not be compatible with what God wants to do *in* us? This is assumption territory.

Have you ever thought that the path you chose would lead you to a different destination? Divorce is not the destination two "love struck" idealists anticipate, and yet 40 percent of every first-time marriage will wind up at exactly that location.[60] How many people have looked to a "religious" experience to solve their anxieties?

Have you ever thought money was the answer to all of your problems? Consider this true story of a Portland man who invented a product that made him wealthy. It seems his new-found wealth allowed him to purchase a gentleman's farm where he could retire and enjoy a simple life. However, along with his newfound wealth came solicitors hoping to sell products and services to him. Fortunately, he had enough money to fence off his property and install a locked gate to keep out the sales people. Unfortunately, his simple life was becoming a little more cumbersome, as now he had to get out of his car to open and close the gate every time he came or left his home.

Eventually, he tired of the exercise and had an electrically controlled gate installed with a remote opener, but he became annoyed at even having to roll down the window to get the signal to work every time, so again he remodeled the gate and had a detector installed to open the gate automatically on the way out.

When this author met him, he was determined to hire a full-time "gate attendant" simply because he had become so bothered by the slow opening and closing mechanism. This man had assumed that money could relieve his life of things that bothered him, but in reality the more money he had, the more things bothered him. This man had lost control of his own desires because of the power of anticipation.

If we assume too much from that which we have control of, how much more do we assume about that which we have no control of? If we have really given our lives to God, by what logic should we assume God wants to do more to honor our desires than build our faith? Our assumptions are a major obstacle to our submission and ultimately to our walk with Christ.

Anticipation was a major obstacle to Israel's obedience. The history we have regarding the Old Testament wars of the Jews is riddled with lessons of the consequences of anticipation. They chose to walk around the land of the giants, assuming they would be defeated, but that just led to more problems. They stored manna while anticipating no provision of God would come tomorrow, and that made God angry. They built a golden calf while guessing Moses was not coming back; consequently many people died. These examples of man's decisions reveal what happens when we *guess* instead of follow, when we *assume* instead of know.

Jesus said "all on the side of truth listen to me."[61] Proper following is our protection against assuming. Following the Holy Spirit and God's teachings insulates us from assumption and introduces us to proper anticipation of God's promises through faith. This is easier said than done in a world where faith often gets equated with claiming promises generated by our lusts and supported by our own assumptions. But we should also mention laziness here as well.

It is easier for us to assume than to know. According to Acts 17:11, the brethren in Berea seemed to catch this concept better than those in Thessalonica because Scripture says: "Now these Jews were more noble than those in Thessalonica, for they received the word with all eagerness, examining the scriptures daily to see if these things were so." This honest follow-through to that which was being taught was said to be "noble." This will require effort on our part. It will take our time, our resolve, and the same eagerness as the Bereans if we are to avoid being duped.

Following our lusts, people or the "kingdoms" of this world, insulates us from God and introduces us to self-fulfilling anticipation. Missing the eagerness to examine God's Word for ourselves is a good indication that we have relinquished our responsibility to know things personally. This is not a good trait for Christians, since assumption is at best passive ownership of knowledge. Assuming things about God is at best passive knowledge of God. Even if our assumptions are true, we do not "own" these revelations in our hearts simply because apathy has been fed by unsupported information. Here it becomes clear: we either choose God or not, and fence straddlers have no protection from this deception.

Any honest seeking of God on our part is an indication that we are wanting to invest in a deeper relationship with Him. It should encourage us to know that we have a way to measure our motives in a real way. Pure motives seek; they do not passively assume. Fortunately, the Holy Spirit helps us to *will* and do God's pleasure (Philippians 2:13). Honest seeking will deliver real finding and not just hopeful anticipation. Here is yet another application of the popular verse: "Be not deceived; God is not mocked: for whatsoever a man soweth, that shall he also reap" (Galatians 6:7). Just plant your own self-serving assumptions, and you will harvest a life of self-serving fruit. Plant a life of following Christ, and you will reap the promises that the Bible claims are " pressed down, shaken together and running over."

CHAPTER TEN

Pudding Without the Proof

Ruse

David, the king of Israel, killed Uriah with the next principle of deception. David killed Uriah with a ruse. Maybe David did not poke Uriah with a sharp ruse or shoot him with a poison one, but it was a ruse that killed Uriah, nonetheless. Here is how it worked. David was trying to hide an adulterous affair he was having with Uriah's wife. David called Uriah home from battle, hoping the Uriah would sleep with his wife and be credited with the already conceived baby. This was the first ruse, because Uriah thought he was invited home from the war for rest and relaxation. He was actually brought home for a sperm donation.

But Uriah declined to be with his wife because he felt it would be dishonorable while a war was raging and his fellow soldiers were dying. Left with no other choice to hide his sin, David sent Uriah to the front lines to "fight." This was the ruse that killed Uriah. Uriah thought he was sent back to war to fight.

Actually, he was sent back to war to die.[62] These are perfect examples of a ruse. The act of apparently doing one thing while actually intending another. We may refer to this as a "hidden agenda" or "false motive," but it is the most uncatchable deception of the lot.

In a fallen world like ours, a ruse or any other principle of deception does not have to be the deceptive intent of an evildoer. It may be that a ruse was nobody's evil plan, but it became a problem because of misguided motives. You really wanted to help out when you volunteered to teach the third grade Sunday school class. But for you it really was never about your desire to the teach kids. Actually, it was easier to say "yes" to the pastor than to say "no," and so now you are the teacher.

Perhaps you did not care for the adult Sunday school class, so you consider this is a better use of that time. Did you tell anybody that this was your motivation for volunteering? If not, these are both examples of a ruse. Your efforts are just an excuse to "skip" out on a boring teaching or appease the pastor. This scenario is far too common and becomes apparent by looking at the problem we have created in our churches today. We have "Sunday school teachers" whose hearts are not prepared to teach. They do not prepare their lessons, they have little passion for their class, and the children can sense it. Nobody's evil intentions planned to kill the life of the third grade Sunday school class, but it is dead, nonetheless.

Both the story of Uriah and this "volunteer teacher" scenario demonstrate that whether a ruse was the plan of a deceiver or just the results of a bad motive, a ruse is hard to spot. Short of a firsthand confession, ruses are "invisible" to our "deception radar" because they are buried within a motive. "Why did you do that?" is the only question that can expose a ruse, and "why" is not a provable concept. As we study this principle of deception, the question "Why did we do what we did?" will surface as a major theme, because "why?" is a huge issue for God. "For the LORD does not see as man sees; for man looks at the outward appearance, but the LORD looks at the heart" (1 Samuel 16:7).

Nobody can always know why somebody else did something. In fact, we cannot always know why we do all of the things we do ourselves. But someday we will be judged for our actions, and our rewards will be tied directly to our motives. God always knows our motives. Even when we cannot bring them to the front of our minds, God sees our hearts. Apparently, our hearts are where our true agendas are kept hidden. Perhaps hidden so deep that we need God's help to even know ourselves.

Psalm 139:23-24 reveals David's understanding of how his own heart may be hiding his true motives from him: "Search me, O God, and know my heart: try me, and know my thoughts and see if there be any wicked way in me, and lead me in the way everlasting." This prayer was David's invitation for God to be first in David's life. This prayer may be necessary if we are to love God with all of our hearts. (Of course, we cannot just say the words to God. We need to actually mean them.) For without a prayer like this, what chance do we have of knowing just what percentage our hearts love God? If we are to love God with *all* of our heart, is 80 percent good enough? Did God really mean *all*? Surely He meant some.

A ruse wiggles its way, invited or not, into our daily choices. But someday our works will be tried by fire, and only motives with value will be left uncharred. You may have prayed or even cast out demons in God's name, but what you did will be weighed against why you did it. When the motives behind our actions get revealed, we may see a very different picture of ourselves than the beautiful self-portrait we have created through our works.

Reading God's Word is just a ruse if it does not involve personal sacrifice and a contrite heart. In other words, as valuable as memorizing the 23rd Psalm may be, if it was just to earn a gold star in Vacation Bible School, it does not demonstrate a heart seeking a relationship with its Creator. Even becoming a pastor without a call may have some value to the individual, but it cannot create a position established and reserved for God alone to fill.

Why do we put money in the offering plate? Is it law, duty, appearance, seed faith, obedience, or an act of love? If Jesus Himself appeared to you personally and released you from any *obligation* of giving, would you still give?

Why do we stay married? This question would be answered quite differently if we could remove all of the obstacles that pressure us to remain faithful in the tough times. Remove the social pressures, the need for support, and the "children" from the marriage equation, and it will be easier to see why who stays with who.

Why do we go to church? In Hebrews 10:24-25, we find the basis for our church meetings: "And let us consider one another to provoke unto love and to good works: Not forsaking the assembling of ourselves together, as the manner of some is; but exhorting one another: and so much the more, as ye see the day approaching." This is our charter, and although we can name other benefits from attending church, "why" we go to church will not be heard from our lips when our actions tell a different story.

Power struggles, splits, judgment, greed, networking, and "soap boxing" are just a few of the results of "our religion" that the world sees. By our fruit it becomes obvious that somebody has an agenda other than promoting love and good works. If we are all going to church for the right reasons, why do so many of us seek out a new church for the wrong reasons?

Why are most of our friends Christians? As Christians we know we are to be separate from the world, but have we separated for the wrong reasons? Are we separate because our love for God makes us peculiar, or are we separate because we are scared?

Scared of temptation. We don't like temptation for ourselves or our children. Scared of evil. We don't want to be around evil, and we prefer to distant ourselves from God's judgment. Scared the world will not understand and agree with us. Since we cannot force the world to understand, believe, or accept our God, we fight the world's "gods" from afar.

Why do we want to be disciples of God? Being a disciple is not hard for us as Christians until we actually begin the work of discipleship. Most, if not all, of us became Christians through very selfish motives. We did not want to perish in hell, we wanted relief from some form of life-controlling problem, or we wanted the good stuff that God promises for His children. But deception confuses us, lies to us, misdirects us, and then sends us on a right mission with wrong motives. We sometimes tend to forget that with our salvation came a mandate to *be* and *make* disciples, not just claim we are one.

If there was only one deception Satan had at his disposal to war against the church in America today, the ruse would be enough. A ruse is in action when our apathy, carelessness, laziness, or personal agenda become hidden beneath our works. A ruse may use props such as marriage, money, or just plain living.

Events and possessions we encounter today are often utilized as unwitting ruses. They decorate the stage of life and become a temptation for us to handle like props on a movie set. Good and necessary things such as food or music tend to slowly evolve from their intended purpose into "gods" in our lives. Food is no longer nourishment when it becomes destructive, and music is no longer a blessing when it becomes an obsession. The motive behind our use of these things will determine the presence of a ruse. We hide our motives from others and publicly play to their expectations. Whether we perform for our peers, our family, our employers, or God, we all have hidden ruses. Everyone has secret motives; it is just the props that change.

We dress for church because it's Sunday, but we do not dress as an act of worship because a ruse has infiltrated our vanity. We pray before our meals, but we have long lost the *adoration* of God for His provisions, because a ruse tells us a quick "thank you" is enough to prove our *gratitude*. We have a hard time knowing ourselves, "why do we like certain people?" "Why do we purchase particular items?" "Why do we spend our time the way we do?"

In his book *The History of the Synoptic Problem*, David Dungan exposes an important clue as to how modern thinking has made this problem worse. Asking the question "why" is less and less on our lips, because as a society we tend to look for "the next" rather than understand our present. David believes that our modern concept of time, which features a continuum of meaningless events, began with the invention of the clock.[63] And with the clock came a new way to think about ourselves.

Although the clock brought much excitement over the ability to tell you *what* time it was, it subtly erased the traditional concept of *"why."* "Before this invention, the passage of time was rarely thought of. Like the biblical view, time was thought of in terms of seasons, such as with the famous passage from Ecclesiastics 3."[64]

For everything there is a season
And a time for every occupation under heaven.
A time to be born and a time to die;
A time to plant and a time to pluck up what is planted;
A time to kill and a time to heal;
A time to break down and a time to build up;
A time to weep and a time to laugh;
A time to mourn and a time to dance;
A time to seek and a time to lose;
A time to rend and a time to sew;

A time to keep silence and a time to speak;

A time to love and a time to hate;

A time for war and a time for peace. (RSV)

We see that time had meaning, and that motive and purpose cycled through seasons of planting and harvest, through the reigns of kings and powers with an incessant temporal rhythm. "Why" was more important than "when."[65] There was a time to do *this* and a time to do *that,* and the clock did not dictate it: your heart and your circumstances did.

Is it any wonder that today *when* we go to church rolls off of our tongues much easier than *why*? Our acts of doing have been clouded by our motives, and our motives alone testify to the deception called a "ruse."

Purpose is being drowned in a sea called "life." Human reason has separated itself from the traditional purpose of community and relations with God, to a featureless, one-dimensional purpose with *personal usefulness* as its goal and *quantity* as its guide.

A ruse dilutes our God-given purpose. A ruse makes sure that our works are isolated from our love of God. This distance between motivated love and our performance allows our self-centered agendas to slip in. This distance is a prerequisite for a ruse. Separation between the sender and the receiver becomes a valuable asset for the success of a ruse. To demonstrate what we mean by this, consider this: Harry Blackstone Sr. found himself utilizing a ruse while performing for a packed Lincoln Theater in September of 1942. As he glanced to the wings of the stage, he saw a fireman frantically gesturing for him to stop the show. Without hardly a raised eyebrow, Harry Blackstone turned to the audience of three thousand and announced, "Folks, my next illusion is so grand this theater cannot contain it. Please follow my instructions carefully so we can file outdoors to view it." The theater emptied calmly under Harry's direction seconds before it was filled with acid smoke and firemen. In this true example of a ruse, "distance" allowed Harry's motive to remain a secret.

Had the audience seen or smelled the trouble (fire), Harry's ruse would have been exposed. Remember, a ruse is just a substituted purpose. If the audience was too close to the real purpose, then a fake purpose would be useless. Likewise, if the audience knew Harry, they would have known he would never have evacuated a theater as part of his show, thereby losing control of his environment and people. All of the crew who worked with Harry knew his act too well to be fooled by this ruse. Distance hides a ruse. Distance from knowing our real circumstances or distance from knowing the character and consistency of those to whom we listen, simply because we don't know what to expect.

Conversely, closeness can sometimes reveal a ruse. Knowing a person well enough to spot unusual behavior is a great asset at a card table, or when raising children. If you could actually get close enough to crawl into somebody else's skin, it would become a lot more difficult for them to purposely deceive you with a ruse. Even our own motives cannot be known once distance has been established between our actions and beliefs. Perhaps this is why the Gospel of John records Jesus giving us this warning: "*Abide in me,* and I in you. As the branch cannot bear fruit of itself, except it abide in the vine; no more can ye, *except ye abide in me.* I am the vine, ye are the branches: *He that abideth in me, and I in him*, the same bringeth forth much fruit: for without me ye can do nothing. *If a man abide not in me,* he is cast forth as a branch, and is withered; and men gather them, and cast them into the fire, and they are burned. *If ye abide in me, and my words abide in you,* ye shall ask what ye will, and it shall be done unto you" (John 15:4-7 emphasis added).

We are not powerless against deception. Fortunately, a ruse is identifiable through the supernatural abilities of discernment.[66] Here, the value of the empowerment of the Holy Spirit in our lives intensifies. Knowing the benefits Satan may gain from the power of a ruse, the gift of discernment should deliver to us new meaning. The Holy Spirit equips us with the abilities to defeat the principalities and power of the air. Without discernment, we are left to historical evaluations and guessing motives from an outcome, even our own. It was discernment that revealed Ananias and Sapphira's motives, so we did not have to wait for a later development to inform us where they erred. On the other hand, it was not discernment that revealed the hidden motive of Simon Magus, and so it required time to expose him.

Simon the sorcerer traveled with Peter and Philip as a baptized believer for a time. It was in Jerusalem that Simon's true motive was learned when his own mouth confessed it. Simon wanted to perform the "giving of the Holy Spirit" to others. Simon's personal ability became his focus, and the Holy Spirit was at best secondary. Paul discerned "a root of bitterness and iniquity" in Simon, but it seemed to have fallen on deaf ears: history doesn't speak well of Simon the sorcerer.[67]

What will history say of us, as individuals and as a body of believers? Through Simon we have been warned to examine our motives. *Why* did we seek salvation in the first place? Did we seek salvation from hell, a drug problem, a failing marriage, poverty, or guilt from our sin? It is dangerous to forget the original conviction that revealed to our hearts that we need salvation from our *condition*, and our condition apart from God is hopeless. Before we saw our need for God, everything about us was without hope. Then one day He gave us hope, and one simple instruction keeps our hope alive and our motives pure. We are to love Him with all of our hearts and all of our souls and all of our might. How easy it is to forget that God is not a means to an end! God is the end; God is love.

This kind of love does not allow room for too much "me theology." This kind of love does not allow us to "improve" the church by arguing over who the choir director is or what hymns to sing. Love like this does not get mad when it is wronged by somebody else's mistake. True love does not argue its method to define a "congregation." Loving God does not allow too much time invested in "getting my fair share." "Give and it will be given to you" is a benefit of a pure relationship with God. It is not a promise upon which we should base a giving practice or lifestyle.

A ruse is the principality that cloaks our hidden agendas with the apparent. "Look," it says, "look at the great results!" But a ruse is not a tool that can change results. A ruse is a tool that hides results. It hides the kind of results that deceive all those who focus on the obvious. A ruse has no problem applauding a person who looks like a well-behaved and articulate disciple of Christ on the outside, who is really a greedy, self-concerned, and powerless soul on the inside.

A true disciple of Jesus is defined by the condition of their heart. This heart seeks to align itself with truth by submitting its own desire to the inspection of the Holy Spirit. In short, this will produce a heart that does justice, loves mercy, and walks humbly before God. Discipleship with any other motive may have value, but it is not best, and it is only a ruse.[68]

CHAPTER ELEVEN

Take a Left at the Tall Brown Cow

Misdirection

Anxious to catch the secrets of professional magician David Copperfield, Dale purchased two tickets to the Paramont theater in Seattle where the master illusionist was to perform. Good seats were purchased early, one for his friend (a local professional magician) and one for himself, in the hopes that Dale's verbal pondering would be answered by his theater companion. "Did you see that?" Dale would ask, "Where did she go?" "Does he use mirrors?"

Trick after trick, Dale was utterly fooled, and trick after trick his friend would answer Dale's question of, "How did he do that?" with the reply, "He did it very well." "Please," Dale would beg, "just one secret, just a hint, please."

Finally, giving in to the pressure of a desperate man who had obviously paid for the tickets just for the right to ask, his magician friend answered, "He does it with the power of misdirection. If you want to catch him, don't watch where he wants you to. Don't follow the spotlight." The timing of his answer could not have been better, as David entered wearing a leather coat driving a large motorcycle onto the stage. The misdirection was classic. David directed attention to the stage center, then over to the right, then walked to the left. What was going to happen? Would David Copperfield disappear? Would he float? A booming sound track of a motorcycle took over for the actual sound of his machine just as the motorcycle was covered, and for the first time in minutes, you knew where to focus your attention. But it was too late. The motorcycle was gone, and you were left watching the back of a man in a leather coat waving his hands in his best "motorcycle be gone" fashion.

However, the man in the leather coat was actually revealed to be a woman, and by the time she had tossed her coat to the stage to expose the double vanish, a theater spotlight was high-lighting David Copperfield sitting atop his bike at the *back* of the theater audience.

Even Dale's friend, the magician, was stunned. "Don't watch where they want you to." Wasn't that the advice? Wasn't that how you beat misdirection? That night everybody learned a lesson. Misdirection started long before anybody knew that it had. It started when the audience submitted to sitting in chairs that all faced towards the stage. Surely everything the audience needed to see would happen on the stage, right? How subtle! Who would have guessed that even "the way things always are" could be used to deceive alert people? Here misdirection utilized the inherent structure of the theater to point people the wrong way! Misdirection always faces us the wrong way.

Misdirected does not necessarily mean totally ineffective or aimlessly wandering. And it does not mean that we are failing to try to discern and obey God's direction. Misdirected does mean that focus gets diverted from time to time. Misdirected does mean that although the general direction may be charted for the masses, very few are on a straight path to get there. Finally, misdirection is not anything new that we should be reluctant to recognize. The multiplicity of Christian denominations in the world today testifies to the fact that somebody's misdirected. Of course, each denomination believes it has a mandate from God, and that may even be true. To some extent a case could be made that denominations are a part of God's plan for the "universal church." We believe that denominations are best understood in the spotlight of history. Consider the following:

Jesus was born right in the middle of a time of gathering. Rome was trying to solidify an empire. The plan was to get a common language, get a good infrastructure for commerce, and to allow all the religious beliefs of the diverse cultures to be accepted. One of the "cultures" Rome had to deal with were the Jews. With over two thousand years fogging our memories, it may be hard to remember that God's people in those days were not Christians. They were Jews. No matter what we may think today of their understanding regarding God's will for their lives, the Jews were as sincere then as Christians are today. In their effort to follow God according to their understanding, the true believers (Jews) practiced what they believed.

In Rome's effort to "gather" the Jews, it soon became apparent that at least four major groups (denominations) would need to be dealt with.[69] Each group (denomination) as sincere as the other, each one with a specific contribution to Judaism and with an identifiable emphasis. First were the Essenes, who might be called the "monks" of the Jews. They were separatists who preserved the Scriptures and effected purity.

A second group of Jews we read about in Scripture were the Sadducees. These were the people who were especially concerned with the temple and all of the ceremony that goes with it. The third group (denomination) of Jews we hear of were the

Zealots. This faction of Jews violently and openly rebelled against Rome and the Roman system or anything that violated their beliefs. They were the ones who insisted on making their last stand at the final destruction of the temple in A.D. 70.

Fourth and perhaps the best known sect of Jews were the Pharisees. Although Jesus had some very harsh words for the Pharisees, they were a product of the times. The Pharisees felt that somebody needed to help the common Jew understand how to apply the Law. Basically, they were the "preachers" of their day. In their efforts to understand the application of Scripture to a changing culture, they became legalists. Their understanding of what God required of them put them in a different position than their other Jewish counterparts. They saw it as their job to confront Jesus. Right or wrong, they were not just being religious as we may be led to believe today. They were a misdirected denomination, but they were sincere.

It does not take much effort to see the same divisions within modern Christendom. The "Zealots" of today (Christian denominations) are picketing abortion clinics, involved with politics, and outspoken from the pulpit on contemporary issues. Today's church has its own "Pharisees" as well, focusing on applying Scripture for the common Christian's everyday lifestyle. "When can I remarry? Is it wrong to be a bartender? Can I watch an R-rated movie? Is smoking a sin?" If not the "Pharisees," (teachers) who will be the authority for our questions?

Today's church also has those denominations that are liturgical, watching over orthodoxy and focusing on the various practices of worship. Finally, today's "Essenes" are our historians and pious prayer warriors, perhaps monks, who practice purity as their mainstay. Obviously, there are more denominations than just these, but can you see how each God-fearing group tends to polarize to a priority? While arranging priorities may be hailed as perfect direction, misdirection may be a more accurate description if we "major on the minors."

James Dobson has helped many people "focus on their family." The very name of his organization speaks of direction (Focus). However, if we allow *family* to become our "god," then the same very positive direction that Dr. Dobson's organization provides to our lives may become misdirection to our *faith*. Is it good to dedicate my entire life to perfecting my marriage? What profit is there for a man who has the perfect marriage but loses his soul?

Is wanting wealth or healing wrong? We are a needy people. We are even needier when we look across cultures and time. Mankind has needed food, water, shelter, information, and protection from disease forever. Is the intensity of a Haitian needing clean water any less intense than our need for a new car? Is the urgency to get the gospel to the Chinese any less urgent than our desire for success and wealth? God is certainly big enough to meet all our needs and heart's desires. But misdirection points our hearts towards the wrong priorities and may have us looking to have our needs met the wrong way.

Is it wrong to plan my life around the doctrines of the future? Are we reading Revelation in our newspapers? Should we spread the warning to prepare for the end? Should we be sending money to the "Save Israel fund"? Does seed faith really work? Misdirection does not care how you invest your time or money as long as your priorities are focused on earthly, personal concerns. Whether born of mild curiosity or intense passion, questions like these will indicate the direction in which our lives are heading. Answer these questions as you like, but you will not find direction here because these questions reveal misdirection, if they replace God as our focus. Self-based religious belief systems can misdirect us all when we seek to leverage our relationship with Christ for our own "noble" agendas while labeling them "God's leading."

How come the Bible seems to offer so much but deliver so little?[70] The answer is misdirection. We are doing the wrong things at the wrong times, the right things at the wrong times, and the wrong things at the right time. There is a time, a right time to address the issues tabled by the Essenes, to worship like the Sadducees, to learn from the Pharisees, to fight like the Zealots. There is a place in our schedules to focus on the family and to pray for healing. We will be wise to know the signs that God has established to remind us that He is in control. But true direction will not let these things displace our original "call."

Direction comes when we acknowledge Christ in *all* our ways. We should learn from those who failed to perfectly get it right. We should not shake our fingers at the Pharisees and say "take that" when we read Jesus' reprimands. Jesus had harsh words for many people with flawed understandings, but Jesus still loved those people. Peter must have been startled when Jesus declared, "Get behind me Satan." How would you feel if Jesus spoke directly to you and said, "It is a wicked generation that needs a sign"? Or if Jesus informed you at your father's old age, "You should let the dead bury the dead"? Jesus' words need to be kept in context for the purpose He intended. Misdirection will utilize His words to pat our own backs, because He did not say those things to us. Or worse, we are misdirected by His teachings altogether.

Would you be surprised to discover that there is no record that the word "grace" was ever spoken by Jesus? In fact, if the corrective *direction* of Jesus' words are not carefully taken in context, *misdirection* is spawned. Then the Gospel's message of what Jesus had come to do is lost, and a tension is created between Jesus' and Paul's teachings.

Paul clearly teaches the doctrine of grace, but Jesus' job was to usher in His kingdom and establish His church. Jesus had some "Old Testament clean up" to do. That meant that the pious followers of God's established laws (the Jews) needed to be shown their need for a Savior. Jesus needed to teach them that the Law had failed to save. The unbelievable requirements Jesus imposed and the harsh language were not because Jesus hated the Pharisees. It was because He loved them. Perhaps Jesus saw them as faithful as He did foolish. After all, Jesus had studied from the very Scriptures the Jews had worshiped. The very Scriptures God had given to them. One thing is for sure, regardless of whether they were foolish or faithful. Jesus was here to bring closure to the system they believed was God's. Jesus' admonition to them to be "even better" was to show them that they (or us) haven't a chance of being good enough.

Just read Matthew's account of the Sermon on the Mount and ask yourself. "Could I?" Jesus may never have said the word "grace," but do not be misdirected into thinking He ever taught a doctrine of works. Jesus *created* grace. Paul taught grace, and God's Spirit administers grace. The Divine initiative is clear. What then shall be the human response?

Consider Martha. The Bible records the account of Jesus visiting Mary and Martha's home. Martha decided to do everything she could to please Jesus. We are led to assume she cooked, cleaned, prepared, offered and was ready to do anything He asked.

Mary was also there with Jesus, but her attention was directed onto Jesus. She was just being what she alone was created for, and so she sat at His feet and listened to Jesus talk. Meanwhile, Martha worked at all the things that were needed.

Eventually, Martha complained, probably because she thought that her efforts were not appreciated by Jesus. But Jesus' response was profound. He told the women, "Only one thing is needed and Mary's doing it."[71] Two women and two reasonable responses to Jesus' visitation, but only one was rightly directed.

This implies that there is a true direction to be sought. Not necessarily Satan's vs. God's. It may be our own direction that competes with the "best" direction. The prophet Jeremiah confirms this to be true. After a short lament of man's self-inflicted failures Jeremaiah declares, "O LORD, I know that the way of man is not in himself: it is not in man that walketh to direct his steps" (Jeremiah 10:23).

Misdirection says, "Do and you will become," while direction says, "You are, so be."[72] We are loved, so we are to love. We are to love God with all of our hearts, and we are to take that love into our communities. We are to make disciples, because we love. We are to understand love from the work of the cross and the instruction of Scripture. Everything else is misdirection.

Life misdirects us. In fact, sometimes it seems that life *is* misdirection, as we earn a living, raise our children, and maintain relationships. How can we possibly be the "spiritual giant" we are told to be on Sunday? How can we keep focused on being a Christian and not just chase doing Christian things? How can we know the difference? Misdirection says, "I will say to my soul, Soul, thou hast much goods laid up for many years; take thine ease, eat, drink, and be merry," while direction says, "Thou fool, this night thy soul shall be required of thee: then whose shall those things be, which thou hast provided?" (Luke 12:19, 20).

In his book *Surprised by Joy,* C.S. Lewis ends with a warning not to blame God that clear directional signs are not forthcoming for those who are lost in the woods of life. Directional signs are a feature of highways and major roads, not a deer trail. If you got off of the road, then you were misdirected. Direction will be more available when you get back on the road. Christians are very vulnerable to misdirection because sometimes we are lost in the woods and do not even know it. We maintain our "camp site" as we sing "We're Marching to Zion," but we foolishly ignore any road that may actually take us somewhere. Not because we are fools, but because we are vulnerable.

We are all looking for direction. It's just that deception makes it so hard to find. And thanks to equivoque we have a limited vision, confusion messes with memories, substitution satisfies our quests, while the authorities we have invited into our lives offer a variety of directions. With misdirection we "claim" scriptures as promises, we memorize passages that contain hope, we even frame and hang scriptures in our homes as an encouragement to us and as a witness to others.

Misdirection is just one more of the ten principles of deception that works to wear us down to apathy. Mature Christians probably have read this far and heard very little new regarding God's expectation of us. After all we have tried to stick to Scripture. It may be one is inclined to think, "no big deal." It may even seem that the authors' perspectives of deceived Christians is harsh as we have presented them. But we are truly worried that most of us are being duped by deception and cannot know it!

What if it were actually true that Satan's power over you really is deception? What if Satan, via deception, could really disarm you of the knowledge of your own vulnerabilities? What if that voice inside of you that says, "I already knew that," is the very voice that keeps you from "owning" the responsibility of "that." What if deception really contains the power to own you? What if Satan's job is to get each one of us underestimating our need for God's day-to-day involvement in our lives. What if misdirection actually has the power to take a major promise and turn it into merely a plaque with which Christians decorate their walls? "In all thy ways acknowledge him, and he shall direct thy paths" (Proverbs 3:6).

CHAPTER TWELVE

Eddie for Freddie With No Time-Outs

Substitution

It was probably one of the most powerful sermons the church had ever heard, not a dry eye in the house. Compelled from the pulpit to respond to the church's duty to minister in their community, nobody was ready to leave when the pastor had ended his benediction. Sensing the need for allowing people to respond, the pastor challenged those who had heard from God in their hearts and were ready to go out and do something to "Stand to your feet." Without hesitation three-quarters of the congregation jumped up in response to the call they had received that morning.

It would seem that the hearts of the people were touched, that the Holy Spirit was saying something to that little church that day. The results were amazing, and most of the congregation was declaring, "Here am I, send me."

Unfortunately, that's the end of the story. We wish we could report that three-quarters of the congregation actually

111

went out and *did* something, but it was not to be. Action was replaced by intent. The conviction for personal action was satisfied by the power of the principle known as substitution. By substituting a sincere public declaration for actually doing what they were originally convicted of, Christians were "benched."

Substitution has hidden from us the Christian obligation. Substitution is the influence that finds us expecting the "church" to do what we are supposed to be doing ourselves. Things like: teach our own children the Word of God, start our own personal Bible study time, personal neighborhood evangelism, or giving care to the needy. Substitution is robbing us of the personal growth that God makes available to us individually. Substitution supports the aberrant disconnects between leadership and teaching, sacrifice and giving, true love and emotion. Of all of the problems we have in the church today, this problem points away from itself. It is switching the focus of problems *for* us in the church with the idea that the problems *are* us. Substitution can so defeat us that we may even lose hope. Hope that we could actually contribute to the Christian obligation. So we throw up our hands and say, "Let someone else do it."

Substitution is a dangerous principle and a powerful weapon of Satan because it can satisfy our feelings. Hence a calling, a motivation, a warning or a word from God may get substituted by a feeling we have sought out instead of a direction we need. Sean Connery played King Arthur in a motion picture entitled *The First Knight*. He was urged by his enemy to divide up land that was neither of theirs to have. When King Arthur was threatened with "Do this or lose the peace you now enjoy," he responded with a profound statement: "Some peace can only be obtained on the other side of war." This is so true: some peace needs to be obtained through a process of obedience and struggles that come from our choices, hard choices that will require sacrifices from us.

The deception known as substitution will never let us learn about sacrifice. Substitution is the principle that seems to urge us to settle now. We are tempted to settle for a form of peace to satisfy some immediate feeling instead of hunker down for a long session of obedience and correction. Some lessons can only be learned on the other side of trials, but substitution will not allow for a test of our resolve.

Not unlike the principle of confusion, substitution affects not only our perceptions but our attention and memory as well. Because of this effect on our ability to process information accurately, our feelings may become the criteria on which we validate our beliefs. In other words, when feelings replace truth, truth is substituted for perceptions. Scripture warns us that someday there will be people insisting to God that they were Christians. They will offer proofs that they believed, that they even prophesied and cast out demons in God's name. But they will hear: "I never knew you." These poor deceived people are in for the shock of their deaths, because what they possess on earth seemed to satisfy them. They substituted a form of Christianity for the "real thing," and it appeared to work for a while. In fact, it even seemed to satisfy up to a point. But a substitute Christianity does not satisfy God's requirements.

This makes understanding what has happened to the "real thing" imperative for us now. What has happened in some cases is that Satan has called in a substitute "look alike" during the game of life without ever calling for a time-out. The switch was swift and subtle, and no attention was drawn to the substitution. Now deceived people mimic proper behavior by doing Christian type things like a religious person instead of having a relationship with Jesus like a justified one.

These people live in a world of "virtual reality." They say the right things, they do the right things, they even feel the right things. They are virtually Christians. They are so close to the real thing that a mere man would not be able to judge them accurately. Who could know that the process of mimicking sanctification was substituted for the requirements of salvation? Something *good* replaced something *necessary,* and these people fell short of the heavenly requirement of adoption.[73]

Probably very few people believe that they can trick God into thinking that they are saved simply by mimicking Christianity. It is far more common that our *hearts* trick us into mimicking Christianity. Mankind was created with a heart that seeks fulfillment, and it will find a substitute if it cannot find the real thing.[74] Church membership, cults, alcohol, work, charities, and fun are a few of the world's stand-ins for God.

"Stand-ins" for God are almost legendary in Jewish/Christian history. Aaron's *bronze calf* stood in for God while Moses was out of sight. We read that *Baal* seemed to be a substitute for a while, and even the Holy Scriptures substituted for a relationship with God.[75] But substituting idols for God was not the only use of this deception. Many things got juggled around as people traded what was required for what was convenient. Just look at the damage substitution can do: Adam traded knowledge of God for knowledge of sin, Israel traded the counsel of God for the counsel of kings, Rome traded Barabbas for Jesus.

Would you have traded wounded and weak sacrifices for good ones? How about substituting "some" money for a tithe? (Ouch!) Have Christians been duped into just substituting a "sinful" life of "sex," "drugs," and "rock and roll," for new life-controlling problems of "apathy," "hypocrisy," and being "piously judgmental"? We even grow accustomed to deception's subtle substitutions, which allow intangibles such as adoration for God to be switched with gratitude to God.

The world has grown accustomed to our substitutions as well. It is not hard to see to whom the world looks in its time of crisis. With the exception of our closest relationships, most of the unsaved look to our professional clergy for answers. As far as the world is concerned, spending some time in church can "answer to" their anxiety better than "answers" they see offered by us. Our original mandate for "aggressive passion" (the Shema) is slowly being substituted for maintained relationships, and the world expects nothing more. Perhaps this story best explains our point:

He was a great Christian man, and I (B.L.) had the privilege of knowing him. It so happens that he was also a pastor in San Francisco. Not just a church pastor, however. He was a pastor of an entire city. He had presided over something like four hundred funerals and described services to me where it was not uncommon to have street life collide with "church life." His wife had a ministry of her own just tending to dysfunctional street people wandering into their services. (One day a "stoned" man crawled up the aisle and tugged at his leg while he was speaking.)

I had just finished speaking to his congregation one evening when I was invited to "see the city" at night via his blue Lincoln Continental. Pastor was old, but his mind was sharp, and as he fitted his sporty riding cap onto the top of his head, I settled myself into the front "row" of his four-wheeled "theater." I saw San Francisco that night. Pushers, users, prostitutes, cross dressers, gangs, probably criminals that had no business on the streets this late. Sometimes Pastor cruised the same streets, the bad streets, a couple times driving slowly and pointing to landmarks and people that had somehow crossed paths with his ministry. For over thirty years Pastor's church on Market Street was home base, but it did not define his job. I will never forget Pastor's words to me that night. The passion in his words revealed to me the heart that fueled his mission. "Bob," he said "Jesus loves these people... and that is why I am here."

Pastor died a few years ago, and one could almost hear the community's collective head turn towards the little church on Market Street. "Who will be the next professional 'lover' of us?" it asks. Indeed, who is called to love the unlovely? The deceptive principle of substitution replies, "Not me. Let's hire someone else."

There is not a lot of pressure from the "world" to change that either. They are used to our professionals showing abnormal passion, but the world, in general, expects the average Christian to just "maintain."

But a relationship with God should not be just "maintained." It should be cultivated. John's revelation to the church warns us of "luke-warmness," and many of us see the signs in our lives that the "fire" is fading. Unfortunately, stirring up the ashes of passion almost seems to become a lesson on substitution itself. We read the latest Christian author, we get more involved in our church, we try to "feel" the worship service. Failing to rekindle the flame, we seek a purpose. Here, substitution has found a willing target, since passion is satisfied when it is replaced by purpose.

Passion for a purpose is good; however, there is a lesson that emerges from the Psalms that might be applicable for us today. David, the author of many of the Psalms, was a man with purpose and passion. His passion for his purpose is legendary. From his willingness to fight the giant, his deep commitment to Jonathan, his loyalty to Saul, it seems everything David did was intense. But David's intensity was born out of his commitment to, his love for, and his fear of God. David's life was not a lesson in personal comfort dished out by the Almighty to a self-centered, weak-kneed believer.

The Psalms revealed his intenseness *against* his enemies and his intenseness *for* his God. David was a man after God's own heart, in our opinion a status he would not have achieved without avoiding a dangerous substitution. David avoided substituting a passion *for* God (emotional enthusiasm) with a passion *from* God (organic purpose).

Avoiding some of the more obvious of substitution's pit falls might best be listed with a friendly reminder of a list of "do nots." First, do not lose your passion *from* God to a passion *for* God. Do not let Sunday School substitute for your personal study of Scripture. Do not let convenient friendships substitute for Christian community. Do not let your mandate to "make disciples" get substituted by your desire to have "heaven" now. Finally, do not let prayer substitute for a relationship with God that incorporates your action.

Thanks to deception, following a list like this is easier said than done. Successfully complying with a list like this is impossible. Ultimately, we will need spiritual help. We need spiritual help because a list like the one above is not really a list with which we could choose to comply with. This is not a list of sins to avoid. If this was a list of sins, we would be dealing with foreseeable and avoidable obstacles. This list of "do nots" represents a list that appears in our "rearview mirrors" as a result of an uncatchable spiritual attack. This spiritual attack is called deception, so by definition we can never see it coming. We might as well have said to you, "Do not let anybody pick your pockets next year." Just as sure as someone will be going home with empty pockets, some of us will sit at home with empty lives, thanks to substitution.

Unlike deception, we always possess the power to discern sin. Unlike deception, we have a free, clear choice to sin or not to sin regarding any situation. Unlike deception, we are held responsible for failing to comply with Scripture's lists of "do nots." But we have no control over a deceiver whose job it is to stalk us. Therefore, when, through circumstances, a deception such as substitution subtly slips ideas into our heads, we need help. We need spiritual help. This help comes when we trust in the LORD with all of our heart. Never relying on what we think we know. We should remember the LORD in everything we do, and he will show us the right way. Let's not think that we are wiser than we are; simply obey the LORD and refuse to do wrong (Proverbs 3:5-7). (Did you catch it?)

CHAPTER THIRTEEN

If I've Told
You Once

Repetition

O f the ten principles of deception, this principle is the most difficult principle to comprehend the danger of. Most of us have learned early on that repetition is good. How else does a first grader learn their ABC's? How does a fifth grader learn their multiplication tables? Without repetition how will an ice skater ever learn her routine or a mailman learn his route? Therefore, we have come to understand that repetition is good for learning. But actually repetition is good for conditioning, and conditioning is a tool for learning. Some conditioning is good (learning our ABC's), and some conditioning is not so good (deception).

Unfortunately, the application of this principle of deception has suckered us personally and stolen our momentum as a community. It has supported bad habits, implanted untrue ideas, devalued our intentions, dulled us to original thought, supported our assumptions, stifled our personal growth, and duplicated our mistakes while providing an environment that is not conducive to necessary change. Like it or not, every day we are becoming conditioned by our environment through repetition. Exposed to the same environment day in and day out, our bodies, our senses, and our reactions are becoming conditioned. This is not always a conspiracy or a result of sin, but a fact of life that is affecting us all. No matter which of our five senses may be responsible for absorbing the conditioning, ultimately our brains will process and draw conclusions from that conditioning. When the conditioning involves repetition, our beliefs become stored deep within our minds.

We will be the first to admit that repetition has its redeeming values for the church. The traditions, sacraments, and the ordinances of God repeatedly bring to our attention the presence of God, and these things are good. Repetition does ingrain the values we are told to remember and uphold. And let us not forget that Shema itself instructs us to teach our children repetitively of the love of God. But let's look at the power of this tool when it is allowed to run amuck throughout the sanctuaries of our sacred institutions.

We fall into patterns: Patterns of behavior, when they are not admirable patterns are often referred to as "ruts." However "ruts" are not necessarily the only ingrained beliefs and behaviors that diminish us. "Ruts" are only the ones we recognize, such as which pew we sit in each Sunday or where we go out to eat after the service. Hidden patterns caused by the principle of repetition can be more subtle and stifling to our Christian walk then just "ruts."

This principle can have us dancing (so to speak) long after the music has stopped. The problem with patterns is that we forget why we started a particular behavior to begin with. Our family life can be affected by thoughtless routines that snuff out organic expressions of love long before they ever have a chance to begin. It happens as subtly as how we choose to talk to each other, how our countenance looks when we listen to one another, or how we purposely budget out time with those we owe it to.

The most basic part of practical church life has also been affected by thoughtless routines—our buildings. A huge percentage of modern church buildings are still being designed by thoughtless routine. The tall ceilings, long narrow rectangle shape, small foyer, and nurseries in the basement are all holdovers from the pre-electricity days. Tall ceilings were necessary for proper ventilation, long rectangles were necessary for sound travel without microphones, and small foyers served a more liturgical crowd. Nurseries have always been a second thought. It has been a relatively few years since some architects have begun to understand that large foyers are needed for fellowship, and parents who drop their kids off at childcare all week feel much better if they are not stuck in a basement on Sunday.[76]

Perhaps worst of all, our prayer life can be affected by thoughtless routines. Through repetition, prayer can become a "habit." It becomes a pattern before we eat and the last thing we do before we go to bed. It is a major reason we tend to forget the beauty of having access to the throne of God. Without specifically looking forward to meeting with God in prayer, repetition can reduce prayer to a ritual as if it were a magical incantation.

Repetition will not extract value from prayer. This is a shame, as there is so much value to be had in prayer. Prayer is a relationship enhancer, a means to an end with God. Repetition treats *prayer* as the object of our relationship with God. But prayer is not our object; it is our method.

Repetition does not let passionless ritualistic prayers identify themselves. Repetition buries these kinds of prayers into our memory as the "norm." Never expecting results, and never seeing any either. Passionless ritualistic prayer may have less value to us than our self-serving ones. Even a wrong intent is sometimes easier to deal with than a mindless habit.[77]

Imbeds beliefs: When constantly exposed to a blitz of similar information, we begin to accept that information as truth. Advertisers also know the power of repetition, and so we buy "Kleenex" instead of facial tissue, "Coke" instead of soda, and "Levis" instead of jeans.

Examples are well known to social analysts: Americans believe that "thin is better," that America is invincible, and that our "rights" are guaranteed. We have been told that there is a Constitutional clause that requires the "separation of church and state" so often that many of us believe it. These are all matters of interpretation, all of which are constantly debated in the arena of public opinion and the courts.

How many ideas are instilled in us by repeated exposure to some piece of information that is not true? Satan, "the little red guy that rules hell," is a common repeated theme in our society. Although it is easy to remember Satan is "not actually red," the average person will probably agree that he "rules hell." However, that too is unscriptural, since God rules everything, including hell, including Satan.

How many people believe that cherubim are cute pudgy little angels? The Bible teaches they are really the "bodyguards" of heaven, that they guarded the tree of life on earth and are pictured at the side of God's throne. Did you know that the three wise men were never at the manger, that there may not have been three of them, that the Bible does not say Jesus was ever in a stable, or that Elijah didn't go to heaven in a chariot of fire?[78]

Worst yet, through consistently doing something wrong, we accept wrong ways as the norm for our lives. Prayer is a good example of this. Many of us learn to pray by listening to others. Over and over again repeated examples of praying teach us that prayer is a list of items that we need which is then addressed by God. Over and over again we learn to mimic our "teachers," thereby perpetuating a style that seems right. Some of us alter our voices, change our common vocabulary, and invoke God's name every other sentence. Day in and day out, year after year, we recite what we have learned to pray instead of praying from our hearts. The result is a relationship with God that is not enhanced, but rather maintained!

Repetition can embed beliefs so deeply we can never be taught truth. "If you're good you go to heaven, if you're bad you go to hell" is such a theme of our world that even many Christians wonder if we are good enough. Repetition is a principle that begins to work on us the day we are born, and by its very nature it gets more powerful with time.

Repetition also dulls our thinking: We tend to believe the things we are told again and again, even when good evidence is in place that could prove just the opposite. Through this principle we can become so gullible that eventually our leaders, our friends, and even the mainstream media have their way with us.[79] The classic example of this is the George Orwell satire, "Animal Farm." It makes the point that when it becomes common to see leaders lie, cheat, and steal, we get used to it. We are not offended, and it becomes just "another way things are."

Repetition is a major cause of dulled thinking, and dulled thinking is the disease that produces symptoms of apathy and gullibility. We tend to get lazy when we find a pattern that requires little effort from us.

Repetition has engraved such a "mouth to ear" system of practicing our faith that we come to get "fed from the Word," and we bring little food with us. The ideas and words are only a Sunday sermon to many. They serve to stimulate our intellects and prick our conscience, but little change is effected. Atonement, sanctification, justification—we hear these words every week, but where is the joy they bring? Repetition has us so used to "mouth to ear" Christianity that sharing the hope of these "big words" becomes lost as an option for us.

Repetition also devalues our intentions: If ever there was a "magic" element to Christian prayer, it would be the transformation of a beautiful instruction[80] into an incantation. It happens every time we mindlessly end our prayers with: "In Jesus' name we pray, amen."[81]

The word "magic" as used in the previous paragraph is a mystical use of the word. It was meant to explain how we believe that without ending our prayer with those exact words, we have not properly prayed. Because of this principle it is easy to believe that somehow those words actually empower our petitions to God. It is true that without the name of Jesus we pray in vain,[82] but what leads us to think that the apostles' examples to "pray in Jesus' name" is satisfied by saying those words at the end of our oration? Repetition does.

Christmas is annual proof that intentions can become dulled by repetition. Christmas now seems to serve man, maybe not for everybody but to many. We may have intended to celebrate the birth of our hope. Christmas was to be one more way to express love for Jesus with all of our hearts, all of our souls, and all of our might. What a great way to be diligent to teach our children of this love, Christmas. But years have taken its toll on many of our outlooks on Christmas. Repetition is at work, hidden beneath the words of the most common greeting that you can hear. Probably heard in every church lobby the Sunday after December 25 is "How was *your* Christmas?" This is a great greeting, but it encourages us to judge how Christmas served us.

The stakes get larger for us to avoid deception when deception is not just an annual event. By pulling an "old play" from the play book weekly, repetition devalues many of our original mandates to hear God and *then* obey. What pastor has not been sucked into the temptation to perform various pastoral duties (i.e., wedding, counseling, preaching) motivated by expectations instead of their original call to love people? The heat of "battle" can necessitate reactions from us that address an immediate need. Repetition is just another deception that suckers us into service with all of the wrong motives. Repetition tends to teach us just to do, to do, and to do again. It is not the best teacher of the "why." Although obedience is good, obedience with intent has a more fulfilling value.

Repetition supports our assumptions: The sky is not falling; it is not going to fall. It did not fall yesterday, and it will not fall tomorrow, right? We know this because we have become used to the sky not falling. This logic seems sound, so let's apply it to our car. "My car is not wrecked; it is not going to be wrecked. It was not wrecked yesterday, and it will not be wrecked tomorrow." This is the kind of logic that repetition loves, it supports our assumptions: "I'm not dead and I'm not going to die, I did not die yesterday, and I will not die tomorrow." Over and over again we become deceived by our deepest beliefs that have no basis in fact. We can believe these things deeply because history is on our side. It is the "so far, so good" mentality, and it is very likely killing us!

Just look around and you will see "the way things are." It does not matter if we are at church learning how to worship or at home learning how to live the Christian life, the way things are tends to be our standard. The principle of repetition strives to just get one more day, just one more historic event under our belts, in hope of having us subconsciously expect the status quo.

How many people believed that the world was flat just because they were always told so? Before the world was proven to be round, Christians had excuses for the Scriptures that said the world is a sphere.[83] What happened to faith? What happened is that repetition of false information became so common that even those predisposed not to believe, believed. Today, how many of us believe that the earth is millions of years old just because we have never heard the other side of the argument? Our assumptions are as big as the sky, as old as the earth, and as deceiving as the daily events of our lives.

Repetition stifles our growth: Many people do not like change. In general we like the familiar, we do not care to "grow," let alone experiment with uncharted territory. While original thinking can break the pattern of "a rut," repetition is not compatible with original thinking. "Ruts" are embedded deep into our ways of thinking, and so breaking out of them becomes difficult to pull off. History (our personal history) has taught us how to just "ride" out deeply grooved "ruts" that bring us personal satisfaction. How else can one explain why America spends such a large portion of its time watching television?

We are creatures of habit, and repetition makes us predictable targets. According to Thomas K. Saville Ph.D.,[84] most women wear jewelry (80 percent own gold chains), the average person has a scar on their left knee, 78 percent of adults have sore feet, the average boy has considered being an animal trainer, the average girl wants to be a teacher, most women feel they are better kissers than their mate, women prefer baths, while men prefer showers, most girls have kept a diary, and most men prefer women with long hair. Given the information one psychologist can know from a few studies, what do you think Satan knows about us after six thousand years of observing the human race? How do you think Satan would use his knowledge against you?

The church in America today is a mile wide and an inch deep. Just as our personal profiles are predictable, so are our abilities. The world sees us as a group of people with common ideas. If you are a Christian, then repetition has supported many assumptions outsiders make about you. For all of the good things they may say, in general we are classified as: judgmental, narrow minded, boring, and unreasonable. If these things are not true about us, then would you agree that only a powerful deception could have supported these assumptions? The question is: is the world so blinded by deception and sin that it cannot see the power and love God instills in us? Or could it be that *we* are deceived? Maybe we meant to grow in the Lord. We meant to be empowered vessels of God's love, but all of our peers are not doing anything much different than we are, and so we just carry on.

Repetition duplicates our mistakes: C.S. Lewis wrote that "a wrong road does not eventually become right."[85] This is true information that has been utilized by professional deceivers since the beginning of time. Once mankind started down the road of wrong choice (Adam and Eve), bad choices have become our greatest downfall. By rewarding a bad choice again and again, we have lost the perspective of our ultimate journey's end. The community, the beautiful music, and the feelings perpetuated by our church institutions have rewarded our proper behavior. But if proper behavior has become our "god," be assured that repetition will not be the one to inform us otherwise. Repetition stifles the searching of our motives. It tends to feed on our patterns of behavior, right or wrong.

Repetition resists change: A byproduct of all of the above negative effects of repetition is the ultimate result of being lulled to sleep: we become lukewarm, unmotivated, and apathetic to change. We cannot help it, for we are controlled by our beliefs. Repetition entrenches patterns of cause and effect that serve to give us our perspective through predictable patterns. The Jewish community of Jesus' day loved its traditions so much that they missed the very thing they were waiting for.

This last principle of deception, repetition, concludes our study on the arsenal of weapons available to the deceiver. We hope the reader has captured the vision that deception is our enemy. It is not just an occasional lie. All ten of these principles can be packaged and repeated as an observable classifiable science.[86] Any magician, con man, pickpocket, or professionally trained deceiver can have this knowledge, and it "should not be tried at home." Unfortunately, home is where most deception occurs. That is because your own heart is better equipped to deceive you than all of the above mentioned deceivers put together. *The heart is deceitful above **all things**,"* and just as we declare "not my heart!" this same verse rhetorically asks us; *"Who can know it?"*

CHAPTER FOURTEEN

Jesus and Me
and the Stuff
I Can't See

I see dead people." This was Hollywood's lead-off trailer for the 1999 movie *The Sixth Sense* that once again pulled potential viewers into the fascination of the unknown spiritual dimension. Today, Harry Potter continues to be a stepping stone for people to pursue their curiosity of the supernatural. And there is a spiritual dimension you know, a dimension that offers a mega-warehouse of shopping options, advertised and packaged by an industry that cares little what we purchase as long as it leaves their store sold. In the book of Acts we learn of a man named Simon, who when introduced to spiritual power recognized the potential of personal gain and sought after it. Acts further records several brothers who attempted to deal with the spiritual world of the apostle Paul with unfortunate results, and today it is not hard to find a prosperous New Age bookstore, television psychic hot line, or a "virtual Christian." The truth is that everybody seems to be looking for the very things Jesus offers, but they look in all of the wrong places and for all of the wrong reasons.

American spiritual seekers are looking for an inheritance in the wrong places and for the wrong reasons. Spiritual power should not be sought out as just another life enhancement. "Virtual Christianity" is not unlike attending the reading of the wills of unrelated dead people, hoping that some secret wealth will emerge because they are dead and you are now rich. "Virtual Christianity" practices a form of the truth, sometimes even seeking spiritual stuff with diligence and passion. But true Christianity is about a relationship, not just an inheritance. If the reader should know anything about deception, it is that deception does not create an environment conducive to achieving Christ's offer of that inheritance. Deception breeds alternatives by hiding our need for God from us. It manipulates truth and will never allow us the ears to hear Jesus' frightening words to us, "I see dead people."[87]

The church is asleep and it cannot wake itself up.[88] In our search for spirituality, we may be just as grossly deceived by our most cherished beliefs as many of our godless counterparts. Even though our traditional Christian ideas are practiced by many of us in a respectful, sincere, and godly manner, through deception we are constantly being deluded. Our testimonies are diluted, our impact on the lost is withering, and even our greatest weapon, our prayers, tends to be self-indulgent.

If you have followed the principles of deception closely, you probably have come to the conclusion that the problem with studying deception is that there is no real way to know if what you see and believe is true. Studying deception creates questions; it does not satisfactorily answer them. We find ourselves asking: What influences have wrongly led us to our views? Can we trust our teachers? Is faith an active force or a perspective? How can I measure my spirituality? Am I the disciple of Christ that I am called to be?

A study of deception is in actuality a study of discipleship. There will never be a better book on discipleship than the Bible, and deception misdirects us from our central mandate from Scripture (to be disciples). Therefore, these fifteen chapters warning of the principalities and powers that distort those truths within the Bible are meant to expose obstacles to our discipleship. Obstacles that manipulate our prayers and hinder our relationship with God's Holy Spirit. Satan knows that without using deception, the Holy Spirit, the Bible, and prayer will be so apparently real to us that we will most likely choose these remedies for our deceitful hearts and *become* disciples of Christ.

So deception plugs our "spiritual nostrils," the nostrils that C.S. Lewis insists should be "kept continually attentive to the inner cesspool."[89] These influences (principles of deception) even offer themselves as a solution for your deceived state, not unlike a bottle of whiskey labeled: "Clean and Sober Medicine." Deception is relentless and circular, so subtly brazen it may offer you a thousand worthless truths for no other purpose than to distract you from a more important perspective.

We would probably agree that the most valuable part of a personal relationship with God is the *eternal* benefits of that relationship. But there are earthly benefits to a relationship with God as well. These benefits include a *personal relationship* that finally makes sense and is delivered as advertised.[90] But there are earthly discipleship mandates for us that go with this relationship. Deceived out of God's best for our lives, we become barely a Christian with only some of the benefits.

Proverbs 23:7 says that what we believe in our hearts we become. Although it is foolish to believe that you are a god and can create your own reality, you certainly can and ultimately must choose what you believe and what you are.[91] The existence of deception explains why so many Christians are powerless, defeated, unfruitful, grossly ignorant of Scripture, and searching for answers that never seem to come. We are participating in salvation, and yet we sit on the sidelines waiting to get the signal to play from the "spiritually talented." We anticipate something good to happen, believing with a pseudo-faith that things will "work out." We boldly declare "God's will be done!" And although we recite these truths, Christians are still an island, we have little impact on the lost, and seldom do our unsaved friends want what we have.

Let's be honest, Do your unsaved friends want what you have because of all the victory and peace your life exhibits?[92] Does your wisdom and knowledge prove God is supernaturally leading your decisions?[93] Do you have an unusual perception of the spiritual realm?[94] Do you or your elders pray for and see the sick healed every Sunday?[95] Does your private worship sound like David's?[96] Our very lives should exhibit answered prayers, faith that has moved mountains, our unspeakable joy, fearlessness, abnormal peace, hope for victory over our problems, and wisdom.

Could you invite a heathen friend into your home to observe the power of your personal relationship with God? This is the heart of discipleship. It is how we measure what we are. We do not point our finger at all of our earthly treasures or at the discipleship type stuff we did. Instead we invite this company of world onlookers into our lives to see what we have by observing how we love.

There is a problem in the church in America today. Deception is still relentlessly attacking the most basic Christian mandate to our discipleship: to love God. For all of the instructions and principles revealed in Scripture, the Shema is the one we must not mess up. For within it is contained the antidote for "virtual Christianity." The Shema was the foreshadowing of our salvation, the basis of our relationship with God, the foundation of any pure motive, the requirement of any unseen promise. The Shema is both a commandment and a privilege, but it is impossible to achieve with a clouded perspective.[97]

No author can deliver in a book a formula to love God. Loving God must be organic and this relationship is a gift that Satan intends to deceive you from. In his book *Letters to Malcolm,* C.S. Lewis suggests this human vulnerability when he writes that the prayer preceding all prayers should be: "May it be the real I who speaks, may it be the real Thou, I speak to."

The author of 1 Corinthians chapter 13 has packaged love as good as it will get. *Now it is up to us to stay focused enough to work out our relationship with God, seeking truth through the Spirit of God within us, to hear the reliable words of Christ.*[98] *This process is the pure motive behind discipleship.*[99] When we get this right, obedience is easy.

Joe looked forward to kindergarten with excitement, passion, and vision. For Joe, his first day of school was the key to "unlock" the impossible to *be* anything! But Joe's first day of kindergarten did not unlock the impossible. It became the impossible. In fact, it was his introduction to a lifetime of failing at seemingly impossible tasks. He didn't stack the blocks, couldn't draw with the crayons, and he couldn't glue the paper or even find the bathroom. Joe's first day was a miserable struggle. When Joe got home he reported that school was too hard and the things he was told to do were impossible for him to accomplish. Joe's teacher noticed Joe's failure as well, and her first impression was that Joe was a problem. In reality, Joe was not a problem, and the projects the teacher required were not too difficult.

Joe's failures were just a result of the vulnerability of his human condition. Joe had been misdirected by another student to the bathroom; therefore, he was looking for the bathroom when his class was stacking blocks. Joe spent all of his coloring time trying to choose his favorite color crayons, and he was confused how to use a glue brush when the glue came in a squirt bottle. Joe was defeated and discouraged by the impossible, so he began to lose any vision beyond "tasks." His life began a pattern of doing instead of "being." Joe only learned on his death bed that stacking blocks and gluing *is* impossible if you are confused and misdirected.

Two thousand years of Old Testament history reveals mankind's inability to fulfill the Shema's requirement. Not because its demands were impossible to achieve, but because just like Joe, mankind is misdirected, confused, and deceived. Obedience seems to be an impossible struggle, and so we fail and sin. Since the wages of sin is death, "Who shall deliver me from this bondage?" is a question we all must answer.

Thanks to Jesus we need not offer blood sacrifices anymore. No need to sneak a turtle dove under our tunics into the temple. The priest no longer suffers the bloody mess or embarrassment of dealing with a major farm animal for his failure.[100] Jesus was not kidding when He declared, "It is finished!" Jesus has delivered us from sin and death. This act of ultimate love is our invitation to a relationship with God based on truth. Truth that needs a pure motive and clear vision on our part. Discipleship is our responsibility in this relationship. Discipleship is not impossible for us to achieve, and it never was.

It is true that submitting our wills to God will at times emerge as acts of obedience and faith, but without organic love we are just noisy religious people,[101] "virtual Christians," blind guides with a form of the truth.[102] Who shall deliver us from our bondage of sin and death? Jesus alone offers *deliverance* from sin and death, and God's Holy Spirit renews and empowers our *vision* daily. *Obedience* through acts of *faith* is our part of the battle against deception, and this *entire package* is discipleship.

Deception will not relent, and by hiding truth, deception offers us a lifetime of struggling against sin or misdirected efforts that may look like discipleship. Without a clear vision of our necessity and ability to please God, without a clear vision of our motives behind our behavior, we will fail to realize our earthly potential. We may become good moralists, we may even win a Noble Peace Prize for admirable behavior, but it is of little eternal value.

If you have stayed with us through this entire book on deception, you may be feeling that a book on grace or blessing would have made you feel a lot better. We agree but make no apologies for attempting to put a name to some of the problems we ourselves have encountered. In the hands of Satan, deception will conceal God, our need for God, our mission with God, and our hope in God.

The ten principles of deception have been grossly underestimated by the church in America today. Deception has been concealing itself behind its own symptoms, silently implying that these ten principles do not even exist. Deception needs to hide so that it does not accept the blame it intends for us to direct elsewhere. Deception is the problem in the Church in America today, not sin, not systems, not pastors, not people. Deception alone stands between Jesus and me and the stuff I can't see, and by definition, deception cannot ever let me know it.

CHAPTER FIFTEEN

Now I Get It

All of a sudden he just was. Seventy-three years was just a timeless event that existed, and Joe had no sense of tomorrow or time. He knew where he was, a promise was kept, and the knowledge of why was realized.

The holes in the man-spirit's wrists took away any thought of speaking. Tears welled up in Joe's eyes, blurring the vision of a crown being offered to him by the Lamb.

Gentle hands wiped the tears from his cheeks, he knew the Master's voice, and so it would be that no introductions were necessary.

"Well done good and faithful servant...well done." Joe couldn't believe his ears. Was Jesus really welcoming him? Jesus Himself! Then a Carpenter's arm scooped up the back of Joe's neck and pulled him into a back-patting embrace as a heavy sigh pressed against his chest. This was heaven.

Remembering the protocol of holy ground, Joe began to slip off his shoes but was interrupted by the sound of five hundred legions of angels clapping at his arrival.

"Leave your shoes on, Joe, you're home," said Jesus.

Joe's lower lip began to tremble, and streams of joy expressed themselves without control. Tears rendered his ability to speak hopeless. He was home. It was a narrower path than he had imagined, but he was home.

There is no time in heaven, so it would not be accurate to say that the angels waited long, but they would have. They always did. The emotions never ceased to amaze them, the tears of joy said volumes, the speechless encounter was always a sure thing, and the wonder of God's love was priceless. Watching a homecoming was unfathomable.

It was the evening and the morning of the only day in paradise, but Joe finally found the ability to say something to Jesus. He didn't look up. He just couldn't look at Jesus without weeping, and so he stared at his own feet as he squeaked with disbelief, "You really love me, you really do."

Jesus' arms still had Joe in a full embrace, so it was natural for them both to turn at Jesus' gesture. It was if a billion eyes were welcoming him as Jesus led him on a path amongst the sea of angels.

"Love you?" Jesus asked. "More than you know. Joe, walk with me and I'll tell you about it." As Joe and Jesus strolled side by side, disappearing into a light that could only be described as glory, the angels knew the story, but they still loved to hear Jesus tell it anyway:

"You see, before the foundation of the world, we said to ourself, let's make mankind after our own image, and so we did. We could have made just anybody, but we didn't, because everybody we made we loved. We decided then and there to create a dreamer, born at a time and place that would aid his anxious desire to achieve a purpose on earth. We always knew he would be special. Joe was just what we wanted…"

ENDNOTES

1. Job 42:5-6.
2. *"You diligently study the Scriptures because you think that by them you possess eternal life. These are the Scriptures that testify about me, yet you refuse to come to me to have life"*(John 6:39-40).
3. Matthew 22:37 and *The Torah* ,A modern Commentary w/ W.Gunther Plaut The Jewish Publication Society 1967.
4. *The Tora,* A modern Commentary Pg. 1364 w/ W.Gunther Plaut The Jewish Publication Society 1967
5. *Pentateuch and Haftorahs*, ed Joseph H. Hertz (Oxford University Press 1929) p.920
6. *Jewish Theology,* Kaufmann Kohler, (New York: Macmillan, 1918) P.90
7. *The Torah,* A Modern Commentary Pg. 1364-65 w/ W.Gunther Plaut The Jewish Publication Society 1967
8. Ibid.
9. Sydney Howard was a world-class runner.
10. Matthew 28:19
11. *Magic by Misdirection,* Dariel Fitzkee Magic Ltd. Lloyd Jones Oakland Calif. 1975
12. Science as defined by the *Oxford English Dictionary.*
13. *Hustlers and Conmen,* Jay Nash M. Evans and Company, Inc. New York 1976
14. Ibid Pg.252
15. *Management Today,* Feb 1997 p70 (1) "A Match Made in Hell" (United Swedish Match Co.'s Ivar Kreuger) Rhymer Rigby
16. *Hustlers and Conmen,* Jay Nash M. Evans & Company, Inc. N.Y. 1976 pg.253
17. *Management Today,* Feb 1997 p70 (1) "A Match Made in Hell" (United Swedish Match Co.'s Ivar Kreuger) Rhymer Rigby
18. Ibid.
19. *Short Changed,* Ralph Mayer , Mickey Hades International, Calgary 1977. A pick pocket exposé with this brazen challenge
20. Jeremiah 17:9
21. Ibid.
22. *The Equivoque Choice*, Jack Dean (self published monograph 1964) Distributed by Mickey Hades International, Vancouver, Canada.

23. "Cold reading" an audience member is an art to itself, requiring years of performing.

24. Romans 8:28.

25. We are more than conquerors. This means we have God's promise to work with all things in our lives if we love Him and are called according to His purpose.

26. One author was taught this on a personal visit to China.

27. The authors do not mean parents and churches should have no authority, but they should not be the intercessor of our faith in God. God must be real and directly the object of our faith.

28. The path of least resistance make rivers and men crooked.

29. Daniel 1:7.

30. *The Two Babylons*, Alexander Hislop, Chick Publications, Ontario, Ca

31. Joshua 2:1.

32. Genesis 27:1-41.

33. *Psychology of Deception,* Jason Randal, Ph.D. Top Secret Productions, Venice Ca. 1982. Pg.. 7-8.

34. Our hearts are deceitful, we see in a glass darkly, God has secrets, to name a few.

35. *The History of the Synoptic Problem*, Pg. 384-390. The author states most scholars have stopped trying to prove the two source theory of the Gospel source, yet it is still the accepted theory.

36. The authors apologize if this seems harsh, but some mission leaders in Seattle have concurred with this observation.

37. Mathew 28:19-20.

38. *The New Jerusalem in the Revelation of John*, Bruce Malina, Liturgical Press 2000 Pg.2.

39. *The Story of Christianity*, Justo L. Gonzalez, Volume 1,Harper Collins 1984.

40. *Letters to Malcolm Chiefly on Prayer,* C.S. Lewis, Harvest Books Harcourt Brace and Co. London 1964 Pg.99.

41. John Bray a Baptist pastor and evangelist (suggests that Elijah did not die but was simply removed to another location).

42. As an example "Zion" as pronounced by most Americans is a Hebrew swear word. Hebrew speaking Israelies pronounce it *Tszon*.

43. You cannot learn proper worship from observations, you must worship in spirit and in truth.

44. *The Screwtape Letters,* C.S. Lewis Distributed by Fleming H. Revell (Baker Books) Grand Rapids, MI 1993 Pg. 21.

45. *Psychology of Deception,* Jason Randal, Ph.D. Top Secret Productions,Venice Ca. 1982.

46. *Magic by Misdirection,* Dariel Fitzkee Magic Ltd. Lloyd Jones Oakland Calif. 1975 pg. 34.

47. Dariel Fitzkee claims; that the real secrets of magic lie in the skill of the performer to influence the mind of the spectator utilizing the principles of deception. *Magic By Misdirection*, pg. 33.

48. *The Pick Pocketing Secrets of Mark Raffels*, Mark Raffels; Tharet Printing works, Kent, England, 1982 Limited edition #455.

49. Ibid.

50. *People's New Testament Commentary*, Regarding Acts 19:40.

51. Police training as related by Captain Vic Piersol U.W. Seattle police dept.

52. *The Screwtape Letters*. C.S. Lewis Distributed by Fleming H. Revell (Baker Books) Grand Rapids, MI 1993 Pg.115. The actual quote was " Success here depends on confusing him."

53. This is the story revealed through 4000 years of history found within the Bible

54. Malcolm Smith has been a major teacher of this view, it presupposes the era of the Jews to be past.

55. John Bray (This view has the events of Revelation fulfilled in A.D. 70).

56. Gleason Archer (This is the most common evangelical view).

57. Jonathan Edwards (A rare and more difficult view to defend).

58. In Revelation, the symbol of John eating the scroll reveals this instruction.

59. *The Rapture*, G.L.Archer, Jr. Paul Feinberg, Douglas Moo, R. Reiter, Zonderman 1984 Here we see disagreement even between those who hold to the premillenial view.

60. The National Center for Health Statistics, 1994.

61. John 18:37.

62. 2 Samuel 11.

63. From the German word "glocke" or bell because these early time pieces were put on church steeples with bells to announce the hour.

64. *History of the Synoptic Proble*, pg.152.

65. *The Gift of the Jews*, Thomas Cahill, Anchor Books Doubleday 1998. This author agrees with the cyclical history time mentioned by David Dungan. *History of the Synoptic Problem*, pg.152.

66. Supernatural abilities of discernment through the Spirit, see 1 Corinthians 12:8.

67. Simon is believed to be the "father" of Gnosticism.

68

69. Only three of these were mentioned by the apostolic historian Josephus.

70. This very real question addressed by C.S. Lewis in *Letters to Malcolm Chiefly on Prayer*, pg. 57-58 is a very important concept that should not be taken lightly. See Harvest Books Harcourt Brace and Co. London 1964.

71. Luke 10:42 "But one thing is needed, and Mary has chosen that good part, which will not be taken away from her."

72. James 2:18 "Yea, a man may say, Thou hast faith, and I have works: shew me thy faith without thy works, and I will shew thee my faith by my works."

73. Adoption; see Romans 8:15 and Ephesians 1:5.

74. *The Culting of America*, Ron Rhodes, Harvest House Pub. Eugene, Or. 1994.

75. John 5:39-40.

76. Church Construction Seminar, 2000 John Taylor, Taylor Gregory Architects.

77. See Revelation 3:14-15.

78. 2 Kings 2:11 He went in a whirl wind, the chariot missed him.

79. *Profiles in Deception,* Reed Irvine and Cliff Kincaid. Book Distributors Inc. NY 1990.

80. Matthew 6:9-13.

81. Acts 3:6 sets an apostolic example of praying in Jesus' name.

82. 1 Corinthians 15:14.

83. Isaiah 40:22.

84. *Red Hot Cold Reading*, the Professional Pseudo Psychic, Thomas Saville Ph.D. & Herb Dewey Published: Mickey Hades International, Vancouver B.C. Page 38-40.

85. *The Great Divorce,* C.S. Lewis Harvest Book Harcourt Brace & Co. NY 1963.

86. Oxford dictionary definition of Science, "observable, repeatable and classifiable."

87. Matthew 23:27 "Woe unto you, scribes and Pharisees, hypocrites! for ye are like unto whited sepulchers, which indeed appear beautiful outward, but are within full of dead men's bones, and of all uncleanness."

88. The authors which to credit this saying to Rev. Milton Stewart, as it was a major theme of his teachings and instructions to the church.

89. *Letters to Malcolm Chiefly on Prayer,* C.S. Lewis, Harvest Books Harcourt Brace and Co. London 1964 Pg. 98.

90. C.S. Lewis in *Letters to Malcolm Chiefly on Prayer* seeks to answer this same question.

91. Romans 12:3 and Joshua 24:15 set the stage for an important choice.

92. Galatians 5:22.

93. 1 Corinthians 12.

94. John 10:4.

95. James 5:14.

96. Psalm 42:1.

97. Philippians 2:13.

98. Galatians 5:16-17 But I say,

99. 2 Corinthians 3:18 when we "behold" Jesus we are changed.

100. Leviticus 4:3 The priest that sins must sacrifice a young bull.

101. See 1 Corinthians 13:1 "Though I speak with the tongues of men and of angels, and have not love, I am become as sounding brass, or a tinkling cymbal."

102. Romans 2:20

Duped!
Order Form

Postal orders: P.O. Box 13394
Mill Creek, WA 98082-1394

Telephone orders: 425-486-3111

E-mail orders: bobjobek@juno.com

Please send *Duped!* to:

Name: _____

Address: _____

City: _____ State: _____

Zip: _____

Telephone: (_____) _____

Book Price: $14.95

Shipping: $3.00 for the first book and $1.00 for each additional book to
cover shipping and handling within US, Canada, and Mexico.
International orders add $6.00 for the first book and $2.00 for
each additional book.

Or order from:
ACW Press
85334 Lorane Hwy
Eugene, OR 97405

(800) 931-BOOK

or contact your local bookstore